TRANSFORMING LIBRARY SERVICE THROUGH INFORMATION COMMONS

Case Studies for the Digital Age

**D. Russell Bailey and
Barbara Gunter Tierney**

AMERICAN LIBRARY ASSOCIATION
Chicago   2008

Composition in Berkeley and Antique Olive typefaces using InDesign on a PC platform.

The paper used in this publication meets the minimum requirements of American National Standard for Information Sciences—Permanence of Paper for Printed Library Materials, ANSI Z39.48-1992. ∞

Library of Congress Cataloging-in-Publication Data
Bailey, D. Russell.
    Transforming library service through information commons : case studies for the digital age / D. Russell Bailey and Barbara Gunter Tierney.
       p.   cm.
    Includes bibliographical references and index.
    ISBN-13: 978-0-8389-0958-4 (alk. paper)
    ISBN-10: 0-8389-0958-2 (alk. paper)
    1. Information commons. I. Tierney, Barbara.
    II. Title.
 ZA3270.B35 2008
 025.5'23—dc22   2007040040

ISBN-13: 978-0-8389-0958-4
ISBN-10: 0-8389-0958-2

Printed in the United States of America

12   11   10   09   08   5   4   3   2   1

Contents

Foreword

Do libraries innovate? This was the topic of the Library and Information Technology Association's Ultimate Debate program at the ALA 2007 annual conference. The panelists discussed stirrings of innovation at the grassroots level, the problem of diffusion of innovation across the library community, and the need for a "sandbox" where innovative ideas can be tested.

The book you are reading makes a strong case for the information commons as an example of library innovation (in staffing, in scope of service delivery, and in the library's stance toward the user) and also of diffusion. In *Transforming Library Service through Information Commons,* Russell Bailey and Barbara Tierney demonstrate how a surprising variety of institutions have effectively rolled out this exciting model that blends new technologies and human expertise across newly reconfigured spaces to better help the library user in pursuit of learning. The reader encounters herein such a range of information commons, across such a broad geographic swath, that we must pause to remember that the whole movement started only some twenty years ago.

Bailey and Tierney also are contributing authors to *The Information Commons Handbook* (2006), but the present book is not its stepchild. Where the *Handbook* thematically explores the historical and institutional contexts of IC planning, implementation, and assessment, this book follows the evidentiary trail of successful commons development through a well-presented set of case studies. Nor should this book be seen as just another in the long series of ruminations about "learning spaces" or "the library as place." Rather, this book is about the substance that goes into a commons space. No one doubts that an IC project could be hobbled by a poorly designed physical layout. But the great variety of successful IC floor plans (round spaces, square spaces, angular spaces, diffuse spaces) argues that substance trumps space. There is clearly no single ideal IC spatial configuration. But within the great variety of divergent IC spaces, there does appear to be a convergent paradigm of IC substance. That substance is delineated in this book.

In her probing review of *The Information Commons Handbook*, Cees-Jan de Jong comments: "The Information Commons is a product of many integrated factors, individual to each institution, which makes it difficult to present a single description."[1] This is precisely the great advantage of the multiple case study approach taken in this volume. The reader can see how the convergent paradigm of IC substance plays out across this variety of institutional environments. And then the reader can better appreciate the significant "lessons learned" offered by those who staff, manage, and evaluate those information commons for their respective libraries. The lessons learned may vary in some details, but common themes do emerge, and in the aggregate they convey the broader realization that the information commons is an expression of this particular period in history when two great long-term eras—the Age of Print and the Digital Age—are grinding against each other like huge tectonic plates. And it also is quickly becoming an expression of our views of the future, for as Robert A. Seal has noted, "The

IC continues to evolve, as it must, in response to changes in user needs and expectations, technology, pedagogy, and society."[2] It would seem, then, that the information commons also may be a plausible candidate for the "sandbox" desired by those LITA panelists mentioned at the outset, especially when managed in collaboration with faculty development and IT/pedagogical initiatives.

I therefore congratulate Russell Bailey and Barbara Tierney for producing a well-conceived and thoroughly researched monograph, applaud ALA for publishing a book that meets a timely need across the profession, and welcome the reader to the innovative substance of *Transforming Library Service through Information Commons*.

—Donald Beagle

NOTES

1. Cees-Jan de Jong, "The Information Commons Handbook" (Review), *Partnership: The Canadian Journal of Library Information Practise and Research* 2, no. 1 (2007); available at http://journal.lib.uoguelph.ca/index.php/perj/issue/view/31.
2. Robert A. Seal, "The Information Commons Handbook" (Review), *Portal: Libraries and the Academy* 7, no. 3 (2007): 389–90.

Case Study Contributors

Abilene Christian University (Texas)
John Mark Tucker and Mark McCallon

University of Arizona
Leslie Sult and Mary Evangeliste

Asbury Theological Seminary (Kentucky)
Kenneth A. Boyd

Binghamton University, State University of New York
David S. Vose

Brigham Young University (Utah)
Michael Whitchurch

University of Calgary (Alberta)
Susan Beatty

California Polytechnic State University
Mary M. Somerville and David D. Gillette

Carleton College (Minnesota)
Carolyn Sanford, Andrea Nixon, Heather Tompkins,
    and Troy Barkmeier

Champlain College (Vermont)
Sarah F. Cohen and Janet R. Cottrell

Dickinson College (Pennsylvania)
Robert E. Renaud

University of Georgia
Florence King and William G. Potter

University of Guelph (Ontario)
Janet Kaufman and Nancy Schmidt

Indiana University Bloomington
Diane K. Dallis and Carolyn Walters

University of Massachusetts Amherst
Anne C. Moore

University of Minnesota–Twin Cities
Caroline Crouse

University of North Carolina at Charlotte
D. Russell Bailey and Barbara Gunter Tierney

St. Petersburg College (Florida)
Susan Anderson, Anne Neiberger, and
Kathy Coughlin

University of Southern California
Shahla Bahavar

University of Southern Maine
Barbara J. Mann and David J. Nutty

University of Victoria (British Columbia)
Joanne Henning

Introduction

Change is a constant in libraries, and the tide of technology innovation rises without ebb. The commons—information, learning, research, and teaching—embodies and nourishes this culture of change, making it imperative that we library and information professionals not only accept but also embrace change and innovation. It is also necessary that we prudently plan, design, and shepherd effective change in resources and services, that we train and educate ourselves and colleagues to lead, guide, and thrive in this culture of change and innovation. In so doing, we not only provide the most effective and influential resources and services for our patrons but, more important, bequeath this natural propensity to productive change as our professional legacy to students, colleagues, and patrons.

Although many of our patrons are "digital natives" of the "digital tribe" (also known as the Net Generation, millennials, or neo-millennials), most library and information professionals are "digital immigrants."[1] We were not "born digital" but have become digital, have immigrated into the digital realm. As digital immigrants, we are well equipped to guide our patrons in both digital and nondigital realms as well as all areas in between—this, too, is part of our legacy.

This volume of case studies was conceived and produced as a gateway to resources that assist and facilitate the professional's work in designing and manifesting effective change in facilities, informational resources, services, and staff. It is intended for several vested groups:

- library, information, and other institutional administrators who are planning strategically and tactically how to improve library services
- library and information staff who are determined to energize and improve their library and information enterprises

- library and information professionals who are seeking ways to become and remain more vital and energized in the next five to fifteen years of their professional lives
- students of library and information studies who are searching for pathways to maximize self-actualization in their careers

This volume serves as a practical guide to enhance and diversify our services and resources; prepare for and facilitate ongoing change and evolution; and provide substantive, richly representative stories from professional practitioners in real settings.

Enhancement and Diversity

For generations, scholars and library and information professionals have developed more deeply than broadly, have educated and trained in a narrow area. This approach is sometimes called the "toothpick-shaped" or "|-shaped" model. Our curricula and libraries have developed similarly in support of the "|-shaped" model. We are now realizing that depth (or even multiple areas of depth) and breadth—broad and multifaceted development—are mutually and vitally important. Technology professionals, for example, have conceptualized a "T-shaped" approach to development, with the vertical part of the T representing traditional science/technology learning and the crossbar pointing to competencies from nonscience/nontechnology disciplines. Likewise, humanist professionals have conceptualized an "H-shaped" professional approach, where the crossbar of the H is field-specific knowledge and skills and the vertical bars relate to areas not specific to field, such as context and community.[2] Library and information professionals have begun to realize that we too must break out of the "|-shaped" model—the narrow and isolated mold—and diversify.

The commons (facilities, resources, and staff) both embodies and facilitates this type of diversification—lateral and vertical integration, the seamless continuum of services and resources, the mutual inclusion of high-touch and high-tech. The commons library professional is both sinew and central force—the "virtualist," "hybrid" professional who develops and continues to renew and grow in numerous areas of relative expertise, embracing all media, multiple subject areas, high-touch and high-tech, as mutually inclusive cultural phenomena. The commons is the framework in which these new professionals teach and thrive. The commons is the teaching and learning laboratory in which information literacy and research education are the curriculum.

Ongoing Change and Evolution

Professional and paraprofessional staff in the field of library and information services can no longer train and tool themselves for static, lifelong careers but rather must constantly evolve. We must be active and dynamic in order to thrive. The commons as teaching and learning laboratory embodies and facilitates effective evolution in services, resources, and staff development. We must transform ourselves several times in our careers to remain current, vibrant, and vital. Although college graduates will likely change jobs ten times in the two decades following graduation,[3] the commons provides to library and information staff and patrons the dynamic arena for such ongoing change.

The commons culture constantly scans for adaptable emerging technologies and integrates them into the repertoire of research and productivity tools available to patrons and staff. In the commons culture, the scan-adapt-scan-adapt modus operandi becomes an integral part of the culture vis-à-vis emerging and traditional technologies and tools.

Substantive Contextual Materials

The academic literature on the commons has been growing since Garrett Hardin's 1968 treatise "The Tragedy of the Commons."[4] The most substantive academic piece on the information and learning commons is *The Information Commons Handbook* (Beagle et al., 2006). The present volume seeks to complement the *Handbook* by providing context-based documentation, evidence, and practical first-person "stories" from twenty diverse and successful commons implementations. Additional content— updates, images, and the like—can be found at http://www.ala.org/editions/extras/Bailey09584.

In their work on the teaching commons, Pat Hutchings and Mary Taylor Huber provide helpful insight into the value and richness of deeply contextual materials presented by commons practitioners. The commons derives its character and value from the notion of property jointly held and usable for collective ends, to foster collaboration and cooperation, and to do so without the need for specific permission. The teaching commons, like the information and learning commons, focuses on practice, and its "practitioners must participate in the effort if it is to have real consequences." The rich representations in the twenty commons stories in this volume provide the details of particular cases, which facilitate and enhance their generalizability. As

Hutchings and Huber note, real stories encourage and create real learning and growth: "People read biographies and autobiographies and use them to guide their own lives and decisions."[5]

We are most pleased to bring to the reader these case studies—these commons biographies— of intelligent library and information professionals determined to provide access to dynamic, vital, and evolutionary teaching and learning laboratories in their particular iterations of the commons.

NOTES

1. Diane G. Oblinger and James L. Oblinger, eds., *Educating the Net Generation* (EDUCAUSE, 2005), http://www.educause.edu/ir/library/pdf/pub7101 .pdf.
2. National Leadership Council, *College Learning for the New Global Century* (Washington, D.C.: Association of American Colleges and Universities, 2007), 16.
3. Ibid., 2.
4. *Science* 162 (1968): 1243–48.
5. Mary Taylor Huber and Pat Hutchings, "Building the Teaching Commons," *Change* 38, no. 3 (2006): 25–31.

## chapter one

Definitions: Information Commons and Learning Commons

Although the terms *information commons* and *learning commons* are often used interchangeably, it is helpful to understand them as different levels of a similar concept. Information commons is the earlier term (dating from the early 1990s) and probably designates earlier iterations of the commons concept. *Media union* and other terms were also used, but these were usually unique to a particular institution.

In this chapter we describe two levels of information commons (adjustment and isolated change) and then two levels of learning commons (far-reaching change and transformational change). Donald Beagle began using these differentiated levels in 2004 (in *Strategic Planning for the Information Commons*), based on recent work by the American Council on Education (in *Taking Charge of Change*).

Information Commons

Generally defined, the information commons is a model for information service delivery, offering students integrated access to electronic information resources, multimedia, print resources, and services. The information commons provides students the opportunity to conduct research and write their papers at a single workstation. It is a single location where one can find resources (e.g., on how to write a paper or troubleshoot a computer or network problem), access numerous databases (both indices and full-text) or the library's online catalog, navigate the Internet to visit websites, and use selected software for research. Tools such as Microsoft Office are available, giving access to file processing and production and complementing robust e-mail, scanning, and other technological capabilities.

Specifically, an information commons (levels 1 and 2)

is *physically* located on one or more floors of a library;

provides *access* to *traditional* library services (often called "high-touch"), including general information, library catalog access, reference services, reserves, circulation, and interlibrary loan;

constitutes a *high-technology-rich* environment (often called "high-tech"), including high-speed networks and public access computers of various types as warranted for patron needs;

provides various resources (hardware, software, support) for what was formerly considered a "computer lab," plus various specialty computer lab configurations (e.g., scanning lab, multimedia lab) *integrated* in terms of space, desks, staff, and training into the traditional library services;

provides a full range of *productivity software* (e.g., MS Office, SPSS/SAS, ArcView, Mathematica/Maple, Adobe Acrobat, Photoshop, OmniPage, Illustrator, Premiere);

makes available to patrons the "electronic continuum of knowledge media" (Donald Beagle, 1999), which is often called the *virtual commons;*

provides various *collaborative* learning and work spaces;

emphasizes Beagle's *continuum of service* (1999): information search and retrieval; processing and interpretation of information; and packaging, presentation, and production in any and all media;

provides near-seamless *integration* from the patron's perspective in terms of space, services, resources, service desks, and staff and incorporates appropriate *cross-training* for many staff;

remains *library-centric:* "owned" and overseen by library staff, even though combining library and computer-lab resources—that is, does not include resources and services that are traditionally from outside of the library;

can be seen (per Beagle and the American Council on Education) in one of two levels:

- *Level 1.* An adjustment—for example, a computer lab with basic productivity software in the library, with resource access and some coordination; minimal space design implications; remains library-centric.
- *Level 2.* An isolated change, including all aspects of the first-level information commons plus additional resources and services—for example, a computer lab with a broad range of multimedia productivity software and formats, access to all resources and extensive integration of space, resources, and staff into the continuum of services, with significantly altered patterns of service, aligned with institutional mission; remains library-centric.

Learning Commons

In general, the transformation from information commons to learning commons reflects a shift in learning theory from primarily *transmission* of knowledge to patrons toward a greater emphasis on *creation* of knowledge by commons staff and patrons and patrons' self-direction in learning. A learning commons includes all aspects of the information commons but extends and enhances them.

Levels three and four in the commons continuum constitute the learning commons. Each of these levels includes all aspects of levels 1 and 2 plus additional resources and services. Specifically, the learning commons

includes all aspects of the information commons, but to a greater extent

- is *clearly and explicitly aligned* strategically with the institution-wide vision and mission—that is, is a dynamic and active partner in the broad educational enterprise of the institution, not just the library-centric enterprise;
- imbues *most of the library* with the integrative (services, resources, staff, desks) perspective;
- includes traditional ("high-touch") and technology-rich ("high-tech") tools and resources;
- provides a fuller range of technological resources, *more seamlessly integrated*
- makes available *more, more varied, and more adjustable collaborative work spaces;*
- extends the "electronic continuum of knowledge media" to emphasize *more creation and construction of knowledge;*

is *not library-centric*—that is, it brings into and includes within the "library" many formerly external functions and activities and extends into the former homes of these functions and activities, such as

- faculty development center or center for teaching and e-learning
- integration of the library into a course management system—WebCT, Blackboard, and the like
- centers for writing, learning support (tutorials), special programs (e.g., honors), learning communities, career counseling
- many collaborative work spaces of greatly varied types, sizes, and adjustability

- greater emphasis on the far end of the continuum—creation and construction of knowledge in institutional repository–and open archives–type activities
- faculty "shared offices," collaborative spaces in library
- may include such less-traditional library functions and activities as exhibitions, readings, performances (music, dance, theater), gaming, lectures, dances (one institution holds its annual fall freshmen dance in the library), panel discussion, institution-wide forums on important/ current/controversial topics, miniature golf, design-to-fabrication laboratories (e.g., MIT's Fab-Labs)

can be seen (per Beagle and the American Council on Education) in one of two levels:

- *Level 3.* A far-reaching change—adding a faculty development/teaching and e-learning center, course management system integration, virtual reference; where the entire enterprise is more collaborative and not library-centric (includes and integrates activities beyond traditional library services plus computer-lab services).
- *Level 4.* Transformational change— adding closer strategic alignment, greater functional integration, including knowledge-creation activities such as an institutional repository (e.g., D-Space, Digital Commons, ContentDM), writing-/ authoring-across-the-curriculum involvement, including an integrated curriculum-support laboratory, greater involvement within and beyond the library of a fuller range of institutional functions and activities in breadth and depth; including some aspect of planning, design, knowledge (and perhaps product) creation/construction/

fabrication (e.g., MIT's Fab-Lab initiative) and not library-centric.

All the various commons iterations—information commons levels 1 and 2, learning commons levels 3 and 4—have many similarities in concept and character, which imbue all commons facilities, resources, and staffing models. All commons emphasize the seamless integration of high-touch/low-tech with high-tech/asynchronous interactions and are strongly and intentionally focused on patron needs. The varieties, permutations, and transmutations of the commons share character and spirit. They differ primarily in robustness and complexity, which are determined by funding resources and particulars of the institutional context.

## chapter two

History and Evolution of the Information Commons Concept

Since the late 1980s, academic libraries in higher education have focused more strongly than previously on patron-centered, learner-centered, user-friendly services. This has been especially true in North American institutions. Models of *integrated library public services* implementations arose in several areas and proliferated through the first half of the 1990s; many of these implementations are known as *information commons*. With the evolution from the Internet (text-based) to the World Wide Web (graphical user interface and hyperlinking) in the mid-1990s and ever greater access to electronic information resources, information commons (or learning commons, library commons, media unions, among other names) have proliferated into hundreds of institutions and continue to develop into more effective delivery of patron services.

It might be helpful to describe the variety of academic programs and patrons that are commonly supported and served in North American academic libraries. The higher education structure and environment of North America differ significantly from those in many other parts of the world, and the IC model emanates from this structure and environment.

North American higher education consists of numerous types of institutions that educate and train students. This education and training include the liberal arts academic programs (humanities, social sciences, arts, natural and earth sciences), preprofessional programs (education/pedagogy, nursing, business, etc.), and, especially in two-year community colleges, many vocational programs (trades, including culinary arts, electrical, auto, technology hardware). Also, each state has a land grant institution (e.g., Texas A&M University) whose educational mission is broad and includes many fields of study: liberal arts, preprofessional, and professional. The library at each institution is expected to serve the full range of student and faculty as its primary patrons, but patrons from the general public usually are considered a secondary patron cohort. Thus, there is a broad range of informational resources (breadth of subject areas and depth of collections), a wide variety of learning styles, and extensive variation in informational needs and readiness to use available resources to meet these needs.

The Association of College and Research Libraries has developed a set of information literacy standards with articulated goals and competencies.[1] That document states that information literacy requires an individual to "recognize when information is needed and have the ability to locate, evaluate, and use effectively the needed information." An "information literate" individual will be able to

- determine the extent of information needed
- access the needed information effectively and efficiently
- evaluate information and its sources critically
- incorporate selected information into one's knowledge base
- use information effectively to accomplish a specific purpose
- understand the economic, legal, and social issues surrounding the use of information and access and use information ethically and legally

It may be helpful to conceive of information literacy as the curriculum information professionals teach within the IC framework. Information literacy and the information commons are complementary organizing principles for effective library work. Information literacy provides intellectual touchstones for understanding and articulating what we can teach our patrons; this is reminiscent of Benjamin Bloom's 1956 taxonomy of educational objectives, cognitive domain: knowledge > comprehension > application > synthesis > evaluation. The IC model helps the design, selection, and organization of resources (informational, technology, and staff) and space for the most effective patron-centered public services.

There is precedent for commons-like integration of services in the United States. Here, community colleges have long provided multiple, integrated services in their libraries (learning resource centers) out of practical necessity (e.g., Maricopa, Estrella, and Mesa Community Colleges in Arizona). Small liberal arts college libraries have integrated services in a similar way, although in these colleges the integration had a bit more to do with the concepts of interrelatedness and interdisciplinarity at the core of the liberal arts traditions than in community college learning resource centers. But in neither of these two cases has the integration of services been conceptually based on learner needs in a high-technology environment. Such a planned, explicit integration is at the heart of the information commons. The commons concept focuses on the provision of research guidance and technical support for patrons who need access to information in all formats, with an ever-increasing quantity of digital resources; access to appropriate hardware and production/presentation software to process the acquired information as needed and support for these hardware/software resources; and appropriate physical spaces to allow, support, and enhance patrons' research and production.

It is important to look briefly at a couple of issues. One is the series of major changes experienced by the world of libraries about a decade ago. Libraries traditionally have had collections at the core of their existence. With the advent of the Internet evolving into the Web, patron services have risen as equally important. Collections are no longer only or primarily housed and waiting in the library just in case, where library professionals can respond to questions about access, use, and the like. The "collection" is a fluid combination of on-site materials (paper, fiche, etc.), proprietary databases, electronic journals and aggregator databases, open-access archives (e-prints, preprints, digital collections, etc.), resources often created at time of need ("on-the-fly"), web catalogs (e.g., http://lii.org), growing "collections" like Google Scholar, Google Print, and Amazon's "search inside the book," and, of course, the full range of search-engine-accessible resources on the Web. To make appropriate use of this vast quantity of variegated information, the learner and the researcher need unique and effective support and service. The value of collections is now balanced by the value of services.

The second issue concerns who our learners and researchers are, what their learning styles and habits are, and how we can most effectively serve them now and in the foreseeable future. Several recent publications bring important focus to these learners, who will soon be our higher education researchers. Several studies on the topic have made us realize the necessity of rethinking, revising, and patterning our services on the changing needs of our learners, our researchers, our patrons: the Net Generation, millennials, neo-millennials, digital natives, those born and come of age since the early to mid-1980s. Library collections and services designed for 1985 or 1990 may not survive the first decade of the twenty-first century unless they adapt. The commons concept provides some insight into possibilities for effective adaptation.

As can be seen from the discussion of definitions in chapter 1, the information commons is an evolving concept that can be implemented in part or incrementally. It does not have to spring fully formed and equipped. Most institutions move in increments; only those that find broad and deep cultural and financial support are able to implement an information commons in its entirety at once.

The primary emphasis of IC services is to provide for patron needs as the evolving nature of the learner is clarified and monitored over time. Complementary points of needs-centered services are, among others

Point of need: Where is the patron in the contemplation and research process—at the beginning, middle, . . . ?

Time of need: Many student (and other) learners and researchers are most active 3:00 p.m. to 6:00 a.m., times when most libraries are physically closed; thus, some 24/7 accommodation is de rigueur.

Place of need: Many student (and other) learners and researchers require services at some place other than the traditional service desk, perhaps elsewhere in the public space or group study rooms, elsewhere on campus, or at home.

Level of need: Variable levels of complexity among, for example, an eighteen-year-old, a graduate student, and a senior researcher must be considered—the services must be adjusted to the varied levels of complexity.

Format of need: Many student learners and researchers are not willing to remain with the format or container libraries have emphasized (i.e., the book, database, journal, or even article); many want only the few most pertinent pages (Amazon's and Google Print's "six-page span") or only the page, graph, or chart, not the larger format.

The information commons focuses most strongly on the needs of the undergraduate patron, although we often see 50 percent or more of our patrons from graduate student and faculty groups. High-level researchers have different needs, which require special tools and environments. Some larger research institutions, notably Indiana University, are developing a research commons complement to the information commons. The research commons will bring research collection access (in whatever format) to individual and groups of researchers, in the same building or widely scattered around the world, in such a way as to allow and facilitate genuine, substantive collaboration, just as the information commons provides this to a more general higher education audience.

The commons concept offers learners, researchers, and information professionals a physical, technological, social, and intellectual place (physical and virtual) to further their various educational and research curricula and activities. The learner and researcher find opportunities for independent, self-sufficient contemplation, research, productivity, and creativity facilitated by the seamless continuum of resources and services in the commons. Though the various iterations of the commons concept in academic libraries are less than two decades old, it is clear that they hold promise of an enlightened era of vibrancy and intelligence in libraries and great hope for those of us who strive collaboratively to produce and share the vision of the dynamic library commons.

NOTE

1. See the information literacy competency standards at http://www.ala.org/ala/acrl/acrlstandards/informationliteracycompetency.htm.

## chapter three

Planning

"A well-planned lesson is already half-taught." This wise teaching adage is pertinent for anyone developing a commons: effective planning facilitates a successful launch and implementation of a commons. This is true for administrators, funders, consultants, architects, and institutional affiliates—professional, paraprofessional, and student. Although approaches and models for IC planning vary widely (and must be adapted to individual situations), useful and usable guidelines and resources are available, which we highlight in this chapter. Each of the case studies in this book includes planning wisdom adapted for the particular institution, much of it incorporated into the "Lessons Learned" sections.

Planning Resources

Much valuable planning information is available via searchable websites of the ALA, the Association of Research Libraries, OCLC, EDUCAUSE, the Coalition for Networked Information, the Council on Library and Information Resources, Project Kaleidoscope, and the like. We maintain a repository site at UNCC and a gateway site at Providence College, which provide rich pertinent files, bibliographies, and links.[1] Several monographs are often cited vis-à-vis commons planning: EDUCAUSE's *Educating the Net Generation* and *Learning Spaces*; the *2003 OCLC Environmental Scan: Pattern Recognition*; Scott Bennett's *Libraries Designed for Learning*; ACE's *On Change* series, especially *On Change III—Taking Charge of Change: A Primer for Colleges and Universities*; among others.

The richest volume on commons issues is *The Information Commons Handbook*. In the *Handbook*, Don Beagle discusses planning at length and in depth, and much that we present here derives from conversations and collaborations with Beagle and other colleagues involved in IC scholarship and ACRL panels and workshops during 2003–2007 (those materials are available on the UNCC and Providence College websites cited above).

Planning Processes

It is paramount that the commons be planned to meet essential needs or sets of needs, both within the library and across the institution at large. It is critical that planning include all phases: strategic to tactical to staged implementation to formative evaluation and revision over time. It is vital that the commons have adequate funding or at least real access to funding. It is important to be aware of how changes the commons represents will be greeted in your institutional environment. It is necessary that the commons and its potential be clearly understood so that its implementation can occur—whether in full or in part, in larger phases or incrementally, quickly (one to three years) or slowly—and still be successful in its impact on services and outcomes.

For needs assessment to be useful, it should consist of a series of multifaceted efforts to determine the prioritized needs, whose needs they are, how enduring or changeable they are, and what aspects of a commons might produce the most influential responses to these needs. Needs of patrons (sources of perceived satisfaction) and of institutional administration (sources of funding and long-term support) are most important. One set of needs emanates from patrons, and it is essential that the data gathered on these needs be demographically representative of the actual or probable patrons. There are numerous examples of needs assessment instruments.[2] Analysis of various data collections (reference transaction transcripts, suggestion box submissions) can be helpful. Focus groups are another means of gathering needs data,

and again *The Information Commons Handbook* describes these for student and faculty patrons. A second set of needs emanates from the institution and key administrators.

For some time we have known the importance of strategic planning as precursor to tactical planning: *why* and *what* before *how* and *when*. Needs emanating from institutional mission, goals, and objectives must be clearly linked to and in strategic alignment with any commons initiative in order for the commons to attract critical funding and support. Focus groups (on campus or as retreats), targeted seminars/symposia/colloquia, and open campus meetings are means to discover and facilitate mutual strategic alignment. The view within the commons must reflect, complement, and jibe with the campuswide view—shared mission and goals enhance success and impact. Strategic planning may take time (months to years), but it is a vital foundation for tactical planning and implementation.

Tactical planning and implementation often flow into one another. Data gathering for these stages often begins with readiness assessments and moves to planning checklists. This is the stage at which many institutions dispatch a scout or site-visit entourage to discover and investigate what other institutions have done and how it might be adapted.[3] Many of these institutions can be contacted via the INFOCOMMONS-L listserv and are eager to share these planning documents and resources.

Resources to help organize and focus planning are also available. CNI posted several for a 2003 ACRL workshop. One is a planning checklist, including preliminary planning, project kick-off, project definition, space, research assessment, personnel, budgets (building, infrastructure, operations), collaboration and partnership agreements, service considerations, and marketing.[4] Another offers an Institutional Quotient Test "designed to help you determine the readiness of your library to plan collaborative spaces" as well as an example of an action plan and other resources.[5]

Most commons initiatives rely on an institutional planning team to determine institutional needs and fit, investigate the concepts, gather information on best practices, report back to constituents, and provide formative oversight and management of the project. Though many members of the team naturally come from the library itself (administrative, professional, and paraprofessional), it is extremely important that nonlibrary participants (institutional administration, faculty, and student body) play key roles. Inclusion of administrative, faculty, and student perspectives, perceptions, and ideas from the outset of the commons project is important if the commons is to serve and be supported by these three groups. Otherwise it remains a library initiative with library-centric limitations. To this we add one brief caveat: although input from library staff is probably the most easily accessible and can be gathered in great quantity, it is often less valuable (valid, reliable, demographically representative) than that from patrons and administration. Strategic alignment with student needs facilitates perceived patron satisfaction (e.g., from LibQUAL+). Strategic alignment with institutional and administrative needs promotes greater likelihood of funding and support.

Planning for Challenges

Another aspect of planning involves the potential effects of and reactions to such change (be it an adjustment or isolated change, or more far-reaching or transformative change) as occurs with commons planning and implementation. These are effects and reactions among the patrons and staff in the library and in affiliate areas, like information technology units, and they should be considered as part of the planning process. *The Information Commons Handbook* refers to these as the "tragedies" of the commons and explains what to expect and how to plan and prepare for them in a way that helps resolve and "transcend" them. The primary "tragedies" are

> *Resource depletion and degradation.* When patrons have access to increased resources, they often use and consume them to the

point of depletion (e.g., printing supplies), so it is important to plan how to control the usage and consumption; when patrons have access to high-end technology and networks, they often download irresponsibly, alter settings, and otherwise degrade the resources, so it is necessary to plan how to safeguard the technology (e.g., with Deep Freeze or other tools).

Resistance (to change). Staff often resist taking on new assignments and tasks "outside" their job description, so one needs to plan for position revisions or restructuring, educating in the value of cross-training and cross-functioning.

Chauvinism. Staff often protect turf from outside their area of "expertise" or from staff lower in the hierarchy, so plans for tiered-services and cross-functioning structures need to be developed.

Success/punished for success. When patrons (students and faculty) come to value and use the technology (hardware and software), space, and support services, they often expect "ever more and ever better," so the commons must plan for the evolving demand for high-value services.

Either/or. As the commons is envisioned, planned, and implemented, there is a constant tension between the extremes, either the traditional high-touch library or the future-oriented high-tech commons, so plans must include both extremes for the value of the full continuum to be developed, revealed, and nurtured.

Dogmatism. Traditional librarians moving into a commons environment often dogmatically prescribe the correct ways and proscribe the incorrect ways, so planning must include options for promoting collaboration among staff horizontally across the library and related areas (especially IT) and vertically between professional, paraprofessional, and student staff. As LibQUAL+ has demonstrated, patron perception preempts what we as library professionals think are the correct or best or preferred ways of providing services; patrons have indicated otherwise by voting with their feet and abandoning the traditional library.

Each set of challenges is manageable if the commons project managers are aware of and adequately plan for them. In most cases, education of staff and patrons is the most effective method for resolution. In the case of "punished for success," it is often helpful to look to student assistants to provide as much support as possible; they are often smart, tech-savvy, relatively inexpensive, and at times can provide better insight into patron concerns and needs than full-time staff.

Planning is of utmost importance—strategic and tactical—and often determines early on the potential for a successful commons. Planning should not be short-changed or oversimplified; it is most effective if given adequate time and resources and pursued as a multifaceted rather than singular endeavor.

NOTES

1. See "library commons" files in the repository at http://digitalcommons.providence.edu and more extensive commons conference files, publications and bibliographies via the gateway at http://library.uncc.edu/infocommons/conference/washington2007/.
2. Santa Clara University provides a valuable example vis-à-vis its learning commons; see http://www.scu.edu/newlibrary/.
3. For extensive notes, images, and gleanings on extensive site visits, see, for example, reports from Joanne Henning, http://jhenning.law.uvic.ca; Susan McMullen, http://faculty.rwu.edu/smcmullen/; and planning documents at Brigham Young University, http://www.lib.utah.edu/misc/bldg_com/docs/04_01_03info_commons_final.pdf.
4 For a useful checklist to be used in planning, see http://www.cni.org/regconfs/acrlcni2003/handouts/checklist.doc for a set of topics an institution can adapt.
5. For a useful action plan to be used in planning, see http://www.cni.org/regconfs/acrlcni2003/handouts/IQhandout.doc and http://www.cni.org/regconfs/acrlcni2003/handouts/actionplan.doc.

chapter **four**

Implementation

Just as effective planning facilitates and enhances success in application, effective commons implementation must flow from planning; many a brilliant commons plan sits unrequited, languishing on the virtual shelf. Focused momentum and sustained energy are required to apply effective planning and often enable successful implementation even when fiscal circumstances and project staff change. Successful implementation does not need to be all or nothing; incremental implementation is common and often more successful in the long run.

David Murray focused on six components of implementation at the January 2004 ALA/ACRL IC workshop in San Diego: configuring and deploying resources; documentation; security; staff training; scheduling for access; and marketing and promotion. This six-part construct provides a helpful modus for delineating successful IC implementation. The following overview of implementation draws on Murray's comments, Beagle's *Information Commons Handbook*, lessons learned from the case studies presented later in this book, and commentary reviewed below from the INFOCOMMONS-L listserv.

The implementation team should include stakeholders from the institutional administration, the library administration and staff, and patrons (faculty and students). Of these participants, institutional administration (funding and support) and patrons (perceived satisfaction) are most important. The participants should not be overly invested in either library tradition (low-tech, high-touch) or technological toys (high-tech, low-touch), since the commons thrives to the extent that it is inclusive of all technologies and all types of interaction. Its offering must be not "either or" but "both and," and the implementation team must reflect and embody this inclusiveness.

Configuring and Deploying Resources

Since it is paramount that the commons project be focused on support of the institutional mission, the implementation team must keep this clearly in mind as the project moves into and through the stages of implementation. The project must include needs of patrons and of the commons staff. The range of resources includes staffing lines, equipment, and furnishings: physical resources (spaces and furnishings—design, renovation, implementation, refinement, maintenance), digital resources (software, website services), human resources (staff and training), and social resources ("political/social capital" for interdependent institutional relationships).

Before a commons is implemented, adequate staffing lines must be available. These staffing lines do not have to be dedicated exclusively to the commons, but they must offer sufficient quantity, variety, and quality of staff to support commons services at a relatively high level of activity (it is rare that a commons does not attract large patronage with its attendant support needs). The staff can be a mix of professional, paraprofessional, and student, full-time and part-time (down to staff contributing only a few hours per week).

A popular commons notion is "ubiquity of computing"—often meaning the exact same computing and ancillary resources across the institution, or at least across the commons. However, ubiquity can also mean similarity at the contact or entrance point, so that the patron can decide at point of contact with the commons' network of resources what he needs to do or select in order to get to the desired resources. The patron is confronted by a familiar entrance point, then chooses the needed resource (hardware, software, network). On the other side of the patron's decision, the commons implementation provides the kind, variety, and combination of resources available: high-end or low-end PC or Macintosh, monochrome or color printing, and so on. The patron enters a ubiquitously familiar "portal" and takes over his informational control. Patrons also expect ubiquity of technology support to complement ubiquity of computing—at the patron's point, level, time, place, format, and speed of need.

Technology resources vary widely. The minimum is usually current hardware (what the typical patron owns), fast web access, and basic productivity packages (e.g., MS Office—patrons expect the full professional version). Beagle gathered data from forty-four commons and calculated average IC computer availability at about 1 percent of undergraduate FTE. He noted that "'smaller' institutions, FTE <5,000, trend toward a higher ratio, with total workstations averaging around 2 percent of FTE. When this subgroup is removed, the average for larger institutions dips a bit below 1 percent of FTE, and a few individually fall to half-a-percent of FTE."[1] These data do not, however, differentiate type or variety of workstations.[2]

Access to power should be more robust than minimally needed to accommodate additional resources as the commons evolves. Network resources should emphasize wireless over wired data drops and wireless printers. Digitization facilities are becoming de rigueur, and patrons expect at least minimal scanning, digital multimedia, and audio/video conversion and editing resources, including Macintosh (preferably Intel) computers.

Printing and alternatives to printing are a common issue. Pay-for-print is commons-compliant (avoids waste), as is access to digital/electronic storage on network servers, floppy disk, CD-R/W, DVD-R/W, or thumb/flash drives. Many commons now vend storage devices, at times via machines in collaboration with the institution or bookstore.

Patrons demand a variety of study spaces—from open computing and multimedia areas to collaborative group spaces to quiet and deep-quiet spaces. The spaces should be accessible—preferably

24/5, 24/7, or something similar—and bookable by patrons; and patrons prefer to check remotely for available space and technology resources before committing the time to come to the physical commons. All workstations should have at least two chairs, and double monitors in some cases to improve collaboration.

The spaces and furnishings must feel pleasant and inviting in order for patrons to trust and commit time to the commons as a collection of resources designed to meet their needs. Not all must be new, expensive, and unified in design, but the patron must sense an intention in the design's purpose; shoddy, unattractive, uncomfortable space and furnishings suggest inattention to the patrons' needs and preferences. The implementation team often works from a detailed floor plan (preferably digital and hard copy) or schematics of spaces, technology, variable working areas, cabling and connectivity, and adequate access to resources for both patrons and staff.

If strategic and tactical planning has emanated from the institutional mission and has involved administration and faculty participants, it is more likely that members of the institution at large will collaborate and cooperate to support the commons implementation. This is especially important, for all commons implementations meet unexpected challenges—delays, cost overruns, facilities "surprises" (HVAC, plumbing and electrical, regulatory permits, etc.)—and the goodwill and support from across the institution, up and down the chain of command, often determine success, or at least level of success.

Documentation

For the commons to have a clear, rational, consistent identity, its planning, implementation, policies, and procedures need to be documented. Documentation extends from planning documents and images of before/after evolution to the nuts and bolts of implementation, management, and maintenance. All documentation should be date-stamped to identify various documents and versions of documents. In part the documentation provides the implementation team an opportunity to track progress and record the level and extent of completed components and tasks; in addition, it allows the team to retrace and review work activities in order to find problems and resolve them more efficiently.

Documentation is more cohesive and effective if one or a small editorial team creates, edits, and maintains it. From these documents (e.g., floor plans and schematics, sample equipment purchase orders, technology specifications, projected service patterns and schedules) emanate materials for staff training and PR/marketing of the commons. As the documentation grows, cohesive editorial oversight produces clear, useful, and well-branded materials for staff, patrons, and the institution as a whole. Some of the documentation makes its way into reports (formative and summative), some into guides and interpretive documents (web-based, electronic, and hard copy), some into patron tutorials, and eventually into professional presentations at the institutional level and beyond to commons peers. Such documentation underlies the case studies included here.

Security and Privacy

The commons staff must be sufficiently vigilant in securing facilities and resources. Still, as technology pundits constantly remind us, network security is a notion, not a fact. It is far easier to secure the facilities than the network. Commons staff should expect increased activity (often extravagantly so) when the commons opens, so security vigilance will be needed.

In-house or institutional security officers (or commons staff) can check for legitimate identification, inhibit harassment (property damage, physical, sexual, and secondary harassment via pornography viewing, etc.) and provide resolution to urgent and critical problems. Security cameras and monitoring systems enhance security. Collaborative group study rooms always should have windowed doors to facilitate visual monitoring. Commons staff can also be encouraged to do regular walk-throughs to enhance security and simultaneously increase staff visibility for improved patron service.

Technology security is much more difficult and elusive. We can encourage responsible use of our networks (vis-à-vis illegal downloading, pornographic or otherwise inappropriate viewing), but it is difficult to enforce. Use of image restoration utilities like Deep Freeze or Clean Slate helps to maintain the integrity of the computer images. We can conduct due diligence in informing patrons of acceptable use vis-à-vis copyright law and restrictions, especially when we provide and support scanning and digitization resources, but it is impossible and unpleasant to police irresponsible behavior. Labels on monitors, scanners, and photocopy machines that quote the law (Title 17, U.S. Code) and the ALA copyright website help inform patrons and indemnify your institution.[3]

The most difficult aspect of security concerns network access. Many institutions are open at least in part to the public and allow public log-on, access, and use of resources. Attempts to monitor and control behavior to prevent breaches prove extremely difficult. Required authentication minimizes unwanted activity from unauthorized patrons, but much of the problematic behavior emanates from our authorized patrons—that is where constant vigilance is required.

The most difficult of the network security problems involve wireless networks, which are becoming ubiquitous, especially in commons. Most institutions have a network security office whose task it is to monitor and at least minimize breaches and to track them down when they occur. This requires constant and ever smarter vigilance.

Finally, consideration must be given to security of patron data and patron privacy, in light of legislation, laws, and regulations. For example, the USA PATRIOT Act and other privacy and security laws and regulations have raised awareness and the need for (especially wireless) network vigilance and management of patron data as institutions struggle with government requests for information and with ever greater numbers of citizens using portable wireless devices and exhibiting savvy in gaining network access.

Staff Training

The implementation team needs to plan for staff training—cross-training, tiered training, and regularly updated training. The training must be targeted and tied to likely patron needs, effective and readily available to staff (in person, web-based, etc.), and in some way assessable in order to determine competency. Training must also be available in an ongoing fashion, formatively evaluated and refined, improved, and updated as necessary.

Patrons often come to technology-rich commons environments with technology intuition ahead of the staff. This heightens the need for staff to develop ever greater competency in order to be responsive and helpful ("affect of service") in guiding patrons and providing effective support. Student staff are often technologically more competent than library professionals, even though they (like patrons) lack many of the high-level information literacy research and discrimination skills necessary to produce high-quality research products.

Training developed for staff often can be adapted and used for patrons, especially if it is available to patrons as needed (point, level, time, place of need) in the form of just-in-time tutorials or guides; these are usually best if they are online via website links, or they can be provided by staff when requested (this is especially true of more complex search tutorials and guides).

Finally, training must be ongoing, updated, and adaptive. Resources change, software upgrades are constant, network capabilities change over time, and patrons' needs and preferences are in a state of constant change. What was true and worked for the class of 2008 may be less effective for the class of 2012.

Scheduling Access

A newly opened commons is often inundated with patrons. To accommodate the patron demand, to gather usage data, and to monitor resource usage, it is sometimes necessary to schedule access to resources. Most commons implementations begin with unrestricted access to computer workstations and other technologies, to collaborative group study rooms, and to other unique and popular spaces and resources.

Some commons schedule collaborative group study rooms to two or more patrons for a maximum of one or two hours, requiring identification and the number of participants (to ensure that it is a group of two or more). Patrons can often extend their reservation if there is no other patron scheduled. Some commons allow remote patron scheduling, but management can be difficult, including safeguarding reservations and preventing overwriting and changes, protecting patron identities, and so forth; patrons favor self-reserving of rooms.

Some commons schedule workstations and other technologies for one- and two-hour blocks. Patrons often can extend their reservation if there is no other patron scheduled. Some commons allow patrons to view computer (and sometimes collaborative group study room) availability on the Web to help them manage their work time and schedules; time is often the most valuable commodity for patrons.

Finally, some commons use the circulation module to check out keys for collaborative group study rooms, presentation rehearsal spaces, or special equipment (e.g., analog-to-digital converter). This provides helpful statistical data and facilitates more effective monitoring of space usage.

Marketing and Promotion

Although it is true that a well-planned and well-implemented commons will draw patrons via the informal, grassroots network, marketing and pro-motion enhance popularity and success, which breed satisfaction and greater success. As Murray pointed out, it is important "to identify someone who is going to be your marketing lead person. . . . it might also be the same person who is the managing editor for your documentation," creating cohesive materials for marketing, documentation, patron and staff reference, reports (annual reports, assessment, grant applications), and so forth.[4]

Marketing and promotion should be created for various purposes (for openings, expansions, added services and hours) of various types (brochures, table-top, mail-outs, service menus), and various media (paper, web-based files, looping PPT files). The marketing and promotion materials need to be changed over time to create a sense of novelty and variety. For instance, materials in adhesive plastic sleeves attached to carrels, workstations, and walls can be used over time by rotating them.

Design of a commons brand offers subliminal communication of the commons' suite of resources and services and through permutations can be an active and dynamic medium for marketing and promotion. For example, one library combined tradition and the commons in a name—"Library + Commons"—and used the traditional black-white institutional logo and the color-and-icon-branded commons logo to "brand" all commons resources and services, both physical and digital (see appendix A); all marketing and promotional materials use this unique brand to communicate to patrons. Another library uses library RSS feeds to promote dynamic commons activities and materials. Still another library uses remote digital signage on monitors throughout the campus to market and promote its commons resources and services. In any case, cohesive, integrated materials (form, content, color, graphics) can greatly enhance the impact of marketing and promotional efforts and materials.

One final emerging area is that of social networking tools, in addition to blogs and podcasts: Ning.com, Facebook.com, MySpace.com, and the like.[5] Many individual IC staff and professionals use these tools to organize and communicate their portfolios, services, and blogfiles. ALA uses Second Life for seminars and symposia. A new commons initiative uses Flickr to share, tag, and organize (in albums) a growing library of images from many commons implementations around the world.[6]

An important aspect of these social networking tools is that patrons inhabit and use these spaces for communication; libraries and commons can use them as well for communication, marketing, and promotion.

■ ■ ■ ■

In conclusion, we note that implementation is an extended and usually ongoing process, and that it is paramount that it flow out of the planning phase, begin gently but decisively, and have sufficient support and resources. The implementation team should have dependable leadership—this could be one person or, preferably, a core of coordinators—who move the project from planning into implementation and eventually maintenance and growth. Few commons projects have an end, since, by their conceptual nature, they adapt to patrons' needs and changes in those needs. Not only do many commons projects expand, but institutions with successful information and learning commons projects that have undergraduate students as the target population are now extending the commons upward in complexity and sophistication to support faculty research needs in a growing research commons phenomenon.

NOTES

1. INFOCOMMONS-L, March 13, 2007. INFOCOMMONS-L is an international listserv of IC practitioners with more than six hundred subscribers from more than thirteen countries. The postings range from the prophetic to the prosaic and offer valuable information to anyone with questions about IC issues.
2. For an extended discussion of the number of computers in libraries, see http://www.ala.org/ala/acrl/aboutacrl/acrlsections/collegelibraries/collubs/white_paper_computers_in_libraries_april2006.pdf.
3. http://www.ala.org/ala/washoff/WOissues/copyrightb/copyright.htm#pages.
4. David Murray, "Information Commons Issues and Trends: Voices from the Frontline," ACRL Panel Program, April 12, 2003.
5. See http://www.pewinternet.org/pdfs/PIP_SNS_Data_Memo_Jan_2007.pdf.
6. See http://www.flickr.com/search/?q=Infocommons.

chapter **five**

Assessment

Assessment is a fundamental process in educational, library, and information settings. It is even more essential for commons initiatives because they usually promise more effective, patron-focused, needs-based enterprises requiring significant commitment of resources—funding, time, energy, space, staff—and require a good deal of change on the part of participants. Thus, it is incumbent on commons planners and practitioners to show evidence of the value of the new or enhanced services and resources. The following discussion of assessment follows up on our earlier commons presentations and chapter 9 of the *Information Commons Handbook.* Additional details follow in the case studies (chapters 6 and 7) as well as the "lessons learned" (chapter 8).

The term *assessment* often refers to a snapshot determination of how things are progressing in general and how effective a set of services is. This snapshot use of assessment is what is termed *summative evaluation:* how things look in sum. Assessment that is ongoing and used to refine and improve something is termed *formative evaluation.* We prefer to use these two terms, since *assessment* is the broader evaluative umbrella and less helpful in assessing IC services and resources.

Formal and Informal Evaluation

Although most evaluation is formal, informal evaluation is at least as important and valuable. Most surveys are formal, as are most focus groups, usability studies, virtual questionnaires, and comment forms, although "just-in-time" pop-up/drop-down questionnaires, for example, are less formal. Formal evaluation is usually more time- and resource-intensive in development (e.g., LibQUAL+ and SAILS), processing, and analysis of the data into meaningful results. Useful informal evaluation can be in the form of observations or anecdotal statements from patrons, staff, or administration; patron comments on surveys or comment boxes; or activity statistics like gate count or head count, reservations for laptops, group study rooms, or specialty labs, queries at service desks, and the numbers of authenticated and other user logons. Formal evaluation is certainly necessary and more often used in institutional reports; informal evaluation of the types mentioned above brings useful insight often absent in formal evaluation.

Qualitative and Quantitative Evaluation

Although quantitative data are more readily available and often used, effective evaluation should include both quantitative and qualitative data. Institutional reports prefer quantitative data, which are thus emphasized in our reports. Common and easily available quantitative data include carefully collected service desk statistics, group study room and specialty lab usage data, and gate count or head count (see the example table and categories in *The Information Commons Handbook*). These data are more valuable when they are gathered, reported, and analyzed longitudinally over time.

Qualitative evaluation is often more subjective and thus at times considered less reliable for formal reporting. Nevertheless, qualitative evaluation data are tremendously valuable, especially when used to complement quantitative data. Common types of qualitative data are anecdotal and focused observation, surveys, usability studies, and focus groups.

Needs Assessment

It is common to conduct some form of needs assessment as part of strategic planning. This exercise

provides insight into changing needs and expectations, how effectively the commons (library) is meeting community needs, and possible additional resources and services. A needs assessment also can indicate who uses the library and ways to reach nonusers; how effective staffing patterns, hours of operation, library services, facilities, and resources are; and how they can be improved.

To make a needs assessment optimally helpful, its designers must determine

- a clear purpose for the study with intent to use the results
- who will conduct the assessment
- what methods and instruments will be used and how the assessment will be administered
- what data will be gathered
- how the information will be used

Most IC implementations follow some sort of needs assessment, either in-house or as an environmental scan (e.g., the OCLC 2003 scan and the regular ACRL scans). These broad scans often serve to bolster any institution-specific needs assessment.

Usability Studies and Focus Groups

Both usability studies and focus groups offer opportunities to evaluate IC services formatively. They are often used together. Focus groups should be designed and run first, since they are more formative in nature; usability studies can then document usability at a point in time (summative). Both approaches must be carried out with the goal in mind of increasing usability and effectiveness of services for targeted patron groups.

Assessment focus groups are guided discussions of resources or services to elicit users' preferences, perceptions, and expectations and to determine how well these resources and services are based on patron needs. The focus group should be designed (for validity) and administered (for reliability) by someone other than those responsible for the resources and services (i.e., those with vested interests) in order for it to be objective and thus reliable and valid. In other words, IC staff should neither design nor run the focus groups. Focus groups also should be demographically representative of the patron population. The group discussions are often recorded and the recorded discussions (or transcripts) analyzed for themes and trends. For example, one focus group indicated

the need for additional software (with specifics) on public service computers, that is, they preferred ubiquity of resources on institutional computers;

the need for longer hours of operation, that is, they preferred that more resources be available at time of need, and perhaps that resources be made better and more easily accessible remotely;

the desire for access to refreshments somewhere in the library, that is, they preferred a full-service library;

the desire for staff to be "nicer" and more willing to respond to technology questions, that is, they preferred better affect of service based on patron needs;

a clear purpose for the study with intent to use the results.

A usability study is an assessment of resources or services to determine how readily patrons can use the services, or which aspects are more or less usable by patrons. The usability study should be designed (for validity) and administered (for reliability) by someone other than those responsible for the resources or services in order for it to be objective and thus reliable and valid. Again, IC staff should neither design nor administer the usability study. Study participants should be demographically representative of the patron population. Participants usually are given an articulated series of real-world application tasks, observed (from an objective distance and perhaps videotaped) with the details of their efforts to perform the tasks carefully noted. These observations are then analyzed (together with videotapes) for themes and trends.

For example: one usability study indicated that

patrons had difficulty saving informational files onto a disk (or other storage device) to be transported to productivity machines, that is, they preferred productivity software on research computers; and

patrons became frustrated and confused.

Although data from focus groups can be relatively subjective, they can nevertheless be extremely beneficial in determining patron preferences, perceptions, expectations, and needs as one looks to refine, improve, or restructure services. Data from usability studies are usually more objective than those from focus groups and often indicate minor or major concerns for usability of services for patrons. These evaluative data should be used together with other assessment tools and methods to clarify the value of services to patrons and to adjust and refine services for greater effectiveness.

Explicit and Implicit Surveys

There are no standard surveys explicitly designed for commons assessment. Many institutions have designed their own and share them with commons colleagues. The University of Calgary, the University of Arizona, and the University of North Carolina at Charlotte are among the many institutions whose IC assessment surveys are available for adoption or adaptation. Some of these surveys are available in chapter 8 of *The Information Commons Handbook* as well as from IC staff at these institutions. The UNC Charlotte survey is presented in this book as appendix B. These explicit surveys are improving and are suitable for most purposes, at times with minimal adaptation.

There are also numerous standardized and widely used assessment instruments that measure commons resources and services implicitly. The Noel-Levitz Student Satisfaction Inventory (https://www.noellevitz.com) is broadly administered to college freshmen and seniors and provides institution-wide data in two items ("library staff are helpful and approachable" and "library resources and services are adequate"), with granular detail on "importance," "performance," "performance gap," and "proportionality" (performance as a percentage of importance) with longitudinal comparative data. Still, it is only implicit and tangential to the commons. Other widely used surveys include some commons-related items. The National Survey of Student Engagement (http://nsse.iub.edu/index.cfm) includes only one item related to the library.

There are at least three commons-implicit instruments that broach adequacy of services and resources in the context of student achievement and outcomes; all are based on information literacy. The Standardized Assessment of Information Literacy Skills (SAILS, https://www.projectsails.org, an initiative following the LibQUAL+ model), developed collaboratively by Kent State and the Association of Research Libraries and partially funded by IMLS, is based on ACRL's information literacy guidelines and has settled into production (provides valid, reliable, demographically representative data). SAILS provides institution-wide data that can be analyzed granularly but not to an individual student. ETS's iSkills (formerly Information and Communication Skills Test, ICTL) has been released but is yet to settle into broad use. It provides institution-wide and individual student reports.

A new information literacy measure is in development by the First Year Information Literacy in the Liberal Arts Assessment project group. It focuses specifically on the liberal arts context, created under the auspices of the National Institute for Technology and Library Education. It was developed originally by a collaboration of eight midwestern institutions and is presently available to the institute's 119 participating institutions.

LibQUAL+ provides the most substantive overlap with commons services and resources. It has settled into standard production, is valid and reliable, and provides institution-wide demographically representative data that can be analyzed granularly and extensively. Nineteen of the twenty-two LibQUAL+ 2004 items are commons-related:

Information Control

- making electronic resources accessible from my home or office
- a library website enabling me to locate information on my own
- the electronic information resources I need
- modern equipment that lets me easily access needed information
- easy-to-use access tools that allow me to find things on my own
- making information easily accessible for independent use

Affect of Service

- employees who instill confidence in users
- giving users individual attention
- employees who are consistently courteous
- readiness to respond to users' questions
- employees who have the knowledge to answer user questions
- employees who deal with users in a caring fashion
- employees who understand the needs of their users
- willingness to help users
- dependability in handling users' service problems

Library As Place

- library space that inspires study and learning
- a comfortable and inviting location
- a getaway for study, learning, or research
- community space for group learning and group study

Still, even LibQUAL+ is intended, not for commons environments, but for all library environments.

Until commons assessment and evaluation instruments settle into greater standardization, we must continue to use various methods and approaches—formal and informal, quantitative and qualitative, implicit and explicit—to create a cultural context of assessment. It is not that difficult to acquire and gain insight from various formative evaluative data if the purpose is to better understand and improve services and resources. The greater difficulty is summative evaluation for institutional administrators and budget officials—the final clear and documented picture of commons resource and service success. Although not final documented proof, the cumulative data available through the above means reveal a compelling picture of success where patrons vote with their feet.

chapter SIX

Information Commons Case Studies: Large Academic Libraries

In this and the next chapter, we focus on case studies of twenty information commons in academic libraries both large (10,000 or more students) and small (fewer than 10,000 students). The information provided is based on questionnaires and templates completed by representatives from each library's commons. In selecting these examples, our goal is to present varied instances of respected, mainstream libraries whose IC facilities seem representative and revealing of this service model.

Each case study includes a summary data chart and narrative sections that address such topics as

- location of institution and campus description
- information commons description
- service transaction statistics
- staffing and training
- what's on the desktop
- assessment
- governance
- lessons learned

UNIVERSITY OF ARIZONA

UNIVERSITY OF ARIZONA MAIN LIBRARY

Prepared June 2006 by Leslie Sult (Instructional Design Librarian) and
Mary Evangeliste (Training Coordinator, Information Commons)

Library website	http://www.library.arizona.edu
IC website	http://www.library.arizona.edu/ic/index.html
Carnegie classification	Research Universities (very high research activity)
# Undergraduates	28,368
# Graduate students	7,387
# Faculty	1,502 FTE (teaching faculty)
Highest degree offered	Doctorate
# Volumes	4,844,241
# Periodical titles	36,060
# FTE librarians	51.75 active FTE, 5.0 vacant FTE, 56.75 total
# Other FTE staff	105.75 active FTE, 9.0 vacant FTE, 114.75 total
Library annual budget	$21,723,566
Annual circulation	231,924 circulations and 158,879 renewals
Annual gate entries	1,549,543
IC opening date	2002
IC name	Main Library Information Commons
IC service model type	Partially integrated services
# Computer workstations	267
What's on desktop	Internet browser, proprietary research databases, word processing, spreadsheet, desktop publishing, graphics, mathematics/statistics, multimedia, presentation; for complete listing, see http://www.library.arizona.edu/ic/infocommons-software.html
IC architect	Gresham & Beach Architects, Tucson, Ariz.
Hours	Mon.–Thurs. 12:00 a.m.–11:59 p.m.; Fri. 12:00 a.m.–9:00 p.m.; Sat. 9:00 a.m.–9:00 p.m.; Sun. 11:00 a.m.–11:59 p.m.
IC area	29,000 sq. ft.
# Physical service points in IC	3: IC reference desk, photocopy desk, and multimedia zone service area
Average # IC users in a typical month	90,000
Print reference materials in the IC?	Yes, limited reference materials are available.

Location of Institution and Campus Description

The University of Arizona was founded in Tucson, Arizona, in 1885. It is Arizona's first state university as well as its only land grant institution. The university is one of the nation's top twenty public research institutions and is a member of the Association of American Universities. There are approximately 28,400 undergraduates and 7,400 graduate students enrolled at the University of Arizona. Students can choose from more than 150 undergraduate programs and more than 200 graduate programs. The main campus occupies 362 acres and has 152 buildings. There are another twenty-two buildings on the medical campus. In 2002 the campus was accepted as a member of the American Association of Botanical Gardens and Arboreta and contains more than 500 species of trees.

Information Commons Description

The University of Arizona Main Library Information Commons is housed on the first floor of the main library; it is also a part of the new underground building, the Integrated Learning Center. The Information Commons was created as part of a collaborative venture between the University Library, the Freshman Year Center, the University Teaching Center, and the Center for Computing and Information Technology. The commons space was designed specifically to be a community area that would foster student retention and enable faculty and students to take advantage of emerging technology. The Information Commons covers 29,000 square feet and houses 267 networked computers. At peak points in the semester it is overflowing with students waiting to use computers. Most computers are arranged in pods of six to eight to facilitate group work. In addition to these pods, the Commons offers computers set up in study carrels. In 2004 the Commons became wireless, and in 2006 the University Library initiated a laptop borrowing program. This program helped reduce the number of people waiting to use computers and enabled students to study anywhere in the library.

The central service and focal point of the Information Commons is the Information Commons desk/reference desk. It is located in the center of the Information Commons and serves as the primary reference point as well as technology assistance point for the main library. A small print reference collection is housed near the IC reference desk, which is staffed by two library employees and two student employees all the hours that the library is open. The Express Document Center (i.e., photocopy center), located at one of the commons entrances, provides printing, copying, and graphic support to students and faculty. The Document Center also serves as the pickup location for interlibrary loan books. There is also a high-end multimedia computing area called the Multimedia Zone, described below under "Special Facilities."

Information Commons Service Transaction Statistics

Approximately 90,000 people use the Information Commons each month. The IC desk answers an average of 2,964 questions a month. These numbers include in-person and phone transactions but not chat and e-mail reference, though these are also answered from the desk.

Information Commons Staffing and Training

The IC desk is staffed all the hours that the Information Commons is open (142 hours a week). The desk staff provide traditional reference services as well as intensive software and hardware support. They also answer the telephone, handle e-mail reference, and manage chat reference during all operating hours. Most hours, the desk is staffed by two trained student workers and two trained library employees. The library employees are a mix of M.L.S. librarians and staff. In the past year the library reference model has changed. When the

Information Commons first opened, an average of thirty staff from all departments within the library worked approximately five hours per week to cover day hours. Hours not covered by this group were covered by staff hired to work the desk late night hours (extended-hours staff). Most of the extended-hours staff are half-time employees.

In 2004 the library analyzed the staffing in the Commons and decided to change staffing models so that a smaller group of people spent a larger amount of time at the desk. This decision was made to increase the overall effectiveness of our reference services as well as to save time and money. Thus in the current model a core group of library staff work the daytime hours (9:00 a.m.–6:00 p.m. Monday–Friday), and the extended-hours staff cover the rest. Although the IC desk staffers attempt to answer all research and technology questions at point of contact, we also have a robust electronic referral system to connect students and faculty with their subject specialist librarians.

Currently all new staff and students must attend and pass a set of eight reference and eight technology classes. Reference classes cover how to search the library catalog; introduction to library databases; how to answer frequently asked questions about the library; how to locate electronic and print journal articles; how to conduct a reference interview; how to use Google Scholar; how to locate full-text articles from library databases; advanced library database searching; and how to locate things physically in the library. Technology classes cover how to troubleshoot the printing system and the printers; introduction to Adobe Photoshop and Microsoft Word, Excel, and PowerPoint; how to troubleshoot computer hardware; how to use scanning hardware and software; how to use CD burning software; and how to create and upload web pages using Dreamweaver.

Training is coordinated by one librarian, and modules are taught by a set of ten instructors. These instructors are responsible for keeping their particular modules up-to-date and for creating new training materials and tests as necessary. Training is offered during the spring and fall semesters.

Information Commons
Special Facilities

There is a computer classroom with fifty computers and an instructor's station that is used for information literacy instruction. The computers in the classroom have the same software as the computers in the larger Commons. The classroom is a heavily used resource, particularly during the fall and spring semesters. Its use is scheduled by the library.

There are twenty-five group study rooms that can be used on a first-come, first-served basis. Priority is given to groups of three or more people, but individuals can use the rooms if they are not occupied. The group study rooms are extremely popular with students and are often occupied at all hours. The rooms are equipped with a whiteboard, table and chairs, and a cable jack that enables students to connect to the university network (if they are not connected wirelessly).

The Information Commons also houses the Multimedia Zone. This area is managed and supported by the Office of Student Computing Resources. There are twelve high-end multimedia computers available with more than forty software applications that support users in the creation and development of virtual reality interfaces, digital video and audio, and 3D animation.

What's on the Desktop

In general, Internet browsers, proprietary research databases, word processing, spreadsheet, desktop publishing, graphics, mathematics/statistics, multimedia, and presentation are available. For complete listing, see http://www.library.arizona.edu/ic/infocommons-software.html.

Information Commons Assessment

The University of Arizona library participates in LibQUAL+ annually. The library also conducts an annual survey of customer satisfaction with services offered in the Information Commons and conducts focus groups when the opportunity arises.

It also provides opportunities for ongoing feedback through the use of the Library Report Card, which allows customers to communicate what they like and dislike about the commons services. One librarian manages the Report Card and ensures that responses to users' comments are sent and publicly posted in a timely manner. Finally, question logging is done twice a year for a week to capture questions and answers to the questions received at the IC desk. We analyze the questions for training needs and the answers for quality.

Information Commons Governance

The Information Commons is part of both the Integrated Learning Center and the library. As part of the Learning Center it is collaboratively managed by four campus units: the University Teaching Center, the Office of Student Computing Resources, the University College, and the library. Within the library the Information Commons is managed and governed by the Undergraduate Services Team.

Lessons Learned

- If you build it, they will come.

- Not only will they come, they will come in great numbers.

- But they won't necessarily be traditional library users.

- And they won't necessarily ask great numbers of questions. We were way overstaffed in the beginning.

BINGHAMTON UNIVERSITY, STATE UNIVERSITY OF NEW YORK

GLENN G. BARTLE LIBRARY

Prepared June 2006 by David S. Vose (Head of Reference and Electronic Services)

Library website	http://library.lib.binghamton.edu
IC website	http://library.lib.binghamton.edu/IC/
Carnegie classification	Research Universities (high research activity)
# Undergraduates	14,018
# Graduate students	2,844
# Faculty	769
Highest degree offered	Doctorate
# Volumes	2,313,597
# Periodical titles	14,693
# FTE librarians	25
# Other FTE staff	75
Library annual budget	ca. $10 million
Annual circulation	301,716
Annual gate entries	1,255,826
IC opening date	March 22, 2006
IC name	Information Commons
IC service model type	Partially integrated services
# Computer workstations	170
What's on desktop	Internet, office productivity software, programming, CAD, statistical, media, graphics
IC architect	Binghamton University Architects/Designers
Hours	All hours the library is open: Sunday noon–Friday 8:00 p.m.; Saturday noon–8:00 p.m.
IC area	8,600 sq. ft.
# Physical service points in IC	1
Average # IC users in a typical month	ca. 172,000
Print reference materials in the IC?	Yes, main print reference collection for library is here.

Location of Institution and Campus Description

Binghamton University dates from 1946, when it opened as a branch of Syracuse University. When the college was incorporated into the State University of New York four years later, it was renamed Harpur College. Growing enrollments and a reputation for excellence soon led to the selection of Harpur College as one of four doctorate-granting university centers in the state system. In 1965 the campus was formally designated the State University of New York at Binghamton.

Binghamton University is 50 miles from Ithaca, 70 miles from Syracuse, and about 200 miles from New York City on a wooded hillside near the Susquehanna River. Binghamton's campus includes the Nature Preserve, a 190-acre forest and wetland area with a six-acre pond.

The campus takes pride in its modern library system. In addition to the main collection, housed in the Glenn G. Bartle Library and Science Library, there are the Fine Arts Collection, the Max Reinhardt Archive of theater materials, the Conole Archive of Recorded Sound, the Link Collection, the university and faculty archives, a map library, a substantial rare book collection, a library annex for lesser used materials, and a new library branch located at the College of Community and Public Affairs.

Information Commons Description

Phase I of the Information Commons opened in March 2006, greeting students returning from spring break with a new facility that replaced the largest public computing facility on campus. The Commons is located on the first floor of the Glenn G. Bartle Library. A glass wall separates the library lobby from the Commons, providing visual access and acoustic isolation. Service points in the Bartle Library are gradually being relocated to the first floor, so that assistance for most needs can be obtained soon after entering the library.

The Commons comprises two adjoining rooms, both of which are accessible from the main lobby of the library. One room previously contained the government documents collection; the other room was the location of the reference desk and still contains the reference collection. The documents collection was relocated to a nearby room, also on the first floor. The reference collection was shifted and its footprint reduced to create room for the Commons. In Phase II of the project the reference collection will be further reduced, providing additional space that can be repurposed for computing resources or other services. Phase I of the project occupies approximately 8,600 square feet. A large part of the Commons has an open ceiling that spans two floors, providing an attractive, well-lighted setting with a feeling of openness.

The Information Commons service desk area consists of two desks positioned back to back, one at chair height, the other at counter height. Each desk faces one of the two adjoining rooms in which the Commons is located. The counter-height desk faces a room with approximately one hundred computer workstations. The chair-height desk faces the room that still houses the reference collection in addition to sixty workstations. Reference librarians and student technology consultants staff these two desks. When staffing levels permit, librarians are paired with consultants at each desk, providing ongoing cross-training opportunities, strengthening the relationship between consultants and librarians, and providing seamless service to those who approach the desk for assistance. The Commons service desk is the first point of contact for many students seeking assistance with library research. The reference librarians and student consultants who staff the Commons strive to be approachable and communicate in a receptive and encouraging manner. Reference librarians emphasize research assistance and provide basic IT support. Student consultants emphasize IT support and help answer basic informational questions.

In addition to walk-in and phone service, librarians staff an e-mail and instant messenger reference service at the Commons desk. Librarians, who are members of the university faculty, serve as subject selectors, liaise with academic departments and programs, teach classes, maintain subject web pages, provide outreach to the university community, and contribute to the profession through publications and participation in professional organizations.

There are a total of 176 computers. Of these 154 PCs and 22 Macs, 160 are "full-function" computers with productivity software maintained by the Computing Services and Educational Technology unit. There is one multimedia/scanning workstation for advanced media creation projects. The remaining computers are maintained by the library and provide a variety of functions. There are four catalog-only computers, four Internet-only computers with basic text editing, and six computers used for CD-ROM and numeric data access. Seven printers are located at strategic points throughout the Commons, including one color printer. Printing is available from all computers. Students print using a page quota system. An express print station allows students to send a job to the print queue quickly without having to wait for an individual workstation. A fee-based printer is maintained for nonaffiliated community patrons.

The full-function computers are stationed on two types of furniture arrayed in a variety of clusters that facilitate student collaboration and small group work by providing generous work surfaces and privacy panels. Additional chairs provide adequate seating for groups collaborating around workstations.

The Group Study/Presentation Practice Room with a large work table and whiteboard is available for students working on group projects or for those wishing to hone presentations. The Adaptive Technology Room with two workstations is equipped with specialized hardware and software. The workstations are available for general use, but priority is given to students with special adaptive technology needs who have registered with the Office of Services for Students with Disabilities and have received training on the use of the technology.

Information Commons Service Transaction Statistics

During the initial nine weeks that the Commons was open, we gathered transaction statistics that showed an average increase in patron contacts with library staff of 176 percent. Transactions conducted by student consultants were not tracked. We will revamp the method of gathering and analyzing transaction statistics in order to provide more comprehensive data for assessment purposes.

Information Commons Staffing and Training

Staffing is a joint effort of the Libraries Reference unit and Computing Services Pod Support group. The Commons is staffed 113.5 hours per week by reference staff and 204 hours per week by student consultants, for a total of 317.5 hours. Consultants are supervised by Computing Services and are hired with input from the head of Reference. Since Computing Services professional staff do not work at the IC service desk, librarians working on the desk provide feedback to their supervisor as necessary.

The IC service desk is staffed all hours that the library is open by a mix of sixteen FTE reference librarians/professionals, two graduate student assistants (0.5 FTE), and twenty-three (0.5 FTE) student consultants. During peak hours (noon–6:00 p.m.) a librarian and a student consultant work side by side at each of the two desks. Morning and evening staffing consists of one librarian and two consultants. The desk is staffed from midnight to 3:00 a.m. by a single student consultant. During the remainder of the overnight hours, minimal support is provided by the library's circulation desk.

At the IC service desk, the reference staff are primarily responsible for research assistance and access to resources and services. Student consultants resolve technical problems encountered by patrons, advise on the use of available software, and perform routine printer maintenance (e.g., paper filling and toner replacement). Individuals working at the service desk strive to answer any question about either information resources or technical issues. Although reference personnel have greater knowledge of research and the use of the collections and consultants have greater expertise in hardware, software, and network issues, we expect expertise to diffuse between the members of both groups.

A checklist of baseline knowledge competencies will be used to develop training for all IC staff. Because student consultants work in other computer facilities on campus as well, training designed specifically for the Commons is necessary to ensure high-quality customer service and consultant awareness of basic library tools and resources. A library student employee orientation program is being developed in which consultants will participate to obtain an understanding of the libraries' service culture and standards and important aspects of public service such as approachability and confidentiality. All student consultants hired by Computing Services will participate in this training so that the customer service standards are consistent in both public computer labs and the Information Commons.

In addition, consultants will receive training on library websites and services, the library catalog, our electronic resources gateway, effective web searching, key online and print resources, policies and procedures, other library units and service points, and how to answer basic informational questions, how to conduct a reference interview, and when to make referrals. Student consultants receive initial IT training from Computing Services and their peers. Training is provided on assisting with e-mail, printing, scanning, and the numerous software applications available on Commons desktops. Consultants are not expected to know how to use all available software but rather how to find applications, open files, use Help, capture data, and print. Some consultants develop expertise with specific packages and can serve as a resource for those needing in-depth assistance. Cross-training will be implemented so that librarians and students have the opportunity to sit together and learn from each other.

Consultants are expected to take a proactive role in the continual improvement of the Commons by offering feedback and suggestions. We look to them for advice on how our training programs can be modified to best address the needs of our staff and patrons.

Information Commons Special Facilities

The Information Commons includes a scanning/multimedia workstation for scanning and advanced media projects, the Adaptive Technology Room for special needs students, and the Group Study/Presentation Practice Room. A consulting area with a PC is available inside the IC service desk area so that staff can help patrons in a semiprivate setting. A large computer at the entrance to the Commons displays a visual map of all computers, highlighting the devices that are both in use and available.

The library circulation desk is in close proximity to the Commons and also functions as the service point for interlibrary loan, course reserves, and laptop and audiovisual loans. Nearby on the first floor is also the Data Services Office, which provides support for accessing, manipulating, and analyzing numeric data. This service is staffed by a graduate assistant with oversight by the head of Reference. The Commons services desk frequently serves as the first point of contact for those seeking assistance with numeric data. Three photocopiers are located in the Commons.

What's on the Desktop

All 160 full-function computers provide Internet access (including access to library subscription resources) and a large collection of application software packages (MS Office suite, word processing, presentation, graphics, spreadsheet, database, desktop publishing, mathematics/statistics, programming, integrated development environments, simulation, CAD, project management, statistical analysis, and file transfer utilities). Most of the software is licensed campuswide and is available on computers in other student computing facilities.

Printing is available on all computers. Non-affiliated community patrons may obtain a temporary guest account that provides them access to web browsers and basic text editors. Community patrons may print using a paid copy card.

Information Commons Assessment

We are developing an assessment program for the Commons. Currently we gather feedback through print and pop-up surveys, personal interviews with users, and suggestion boxes.

Information Commons Governance

The Commons opened in the late spring of 2006 as a collaborative enterprise between the University Libraries and Computing Services and Educational Technology with a shared governance structure. Planning and decisions regarding the Commons configuration, services, and support are addressed jointly.

Daily operational oversight of the Commons is the responsibility of the six-member Information Commons Standing Committee, which comprises staff from the Libraries' Public Services Division and the Computing Services Pod Support group. Library reference staff are primarily responsible for providing research assistance and promoting effective access to resources. The Computing Services Pod Support group is responsible for consulting on and providing the computer hardware, software, and network resources available in the Information Commons facility. The committee meets frequently to plan the delivery of high-quality, seamless information and technology services. The Commons is a dynamic academic environment, and the committee strives to be flexible in addressing the changing needs and expectations of the students who use it. Problems, ideas, and suggestions about the daily operations of the Commons are actively sought from students and staff and are used in the planning and management of the facility.

Individual managers are responsible for appropriate communication and coordination for any matters of significance that affect both service groups within the Information Commons. Because the Commons is located in the library building, facilities issues other than those relating to computing infrastructure are addressed by the library.

Lessons Learned

▌ The biggest lesson has been the challenge of blending the services and resources of two campus units with very different cultures: the Libraries and Computing Services and Educational Technology. Each unit has a unique mission orientation and focus. Using the services of an objective facilitator was extremely helpful in the collaboration process. Also, the joint service standards we established for the Commons helped us keep our focus and work together toward the common goal of establishing a high-quality service, research, and computing environment.

▌ No matter how carefully you plan, you cannot anticipate everything. Things such as student expectations and reactions to the new facility, how they use the facility, and how they shape its environment are not always predictable. Communication and marketing can help mold expectations so that the vision for the facility and how it is perceived are in alignment.

▌ Start the planning process early to allow more time for greater input from students.

▌ Design the service desk in a way that is conducive to working side by side with student consultants and that clearly communicates to patrons how the service point works.

▌ Configure furniture so that available workstations are easily visible from the facility's entrance.

▌ As we think about the second phase of the Commons, we are taking careful note of what works best, what could be changed, and what else might be added to enhance the facility. Ideas include the placement of instructional classrooms within or adjacent to the Commons. Because space is finite and there is a constant demand for more student computing capacity, such classrooms could be available for general use except when needed for instruction. Additional group study and presentation practice rooms are possibilities. We may also consider zoning for noisy and quiet use, for short-term and long-term use of workstations, and for individual and collaborative use. Additional equipment might include more multimedia creation stations, SMART Boards for group use, and equipment that facilitates access to digitized materials and learning objects. The inclusion of additional student support services (e.g., paper-writing assistance or tutoring) within or near the Commons would be a real benefit to students, even as small satellite stations with limited hours.

BRIGHAM YOUNG UNIVERSITY

HAROLD B. LEE LIBRARY

Prepared June 2006 by Michael Whitchurch (Information Commons Section Head)

Library website	http://www.lib.byu.edu
IC website	http://www.lib.byu.edu/departs/gen/ic/index.html
Carnegie classification	Research Universities (high research activity)
# Undergraduates	26,928 full-time, 3,314 part-time
# Graduate students	1,484
# Faculty	1,600 faculty, 1,300 administrative, 1,200 staff
Highest degree offered	Doctorate
# Volumes	3,538,205
# Titles	3,398,058
# Periodical titles	27,161
# FTE librarians	73
# Other FTE staff	102
Library annual budget	$24,341,029
Annual circulation	825,744
Annual gate entries	3,221,551
IC opening date	February 24, 2004
IC name	Harold B. Lee Library Information Commons (a.k.a. No Shhh! Zone)
IC service model type	Partially integrated services
# Computer workstations	63 individual, 5 public, 52 group, 4 consultation, 6 multimedia, 2 in study rooms = 132 total
What's on desktop	IE, Firefox, MS Office 2003, Photoshop (Elements)/Omni Page Pro/Adobe Acrobat Pro, Nero, multimedia software, Macromedia suite
IC architect	None; repurposed existing general reference space
Hours	Mon.–Fri. 7:00 a.m.–12:00 a.m., Sat. 8:00 a.m.–12:00 a.m.
IC area	19,250 sq. ft.
# Physical service points in IC	3: Reference, Computer Assistance, Multimedia Assistance
Average # IC users in a typical month	42,596 computer log-ins (does not include numbers using the space to study without logging in)
Print reference materials in the IC?	Yes, but very few. Most have been moved to other subject-specific reference areas.

Location of Institution and Campus Description

Begun in 1875 and first named Brigham Young Academy in 1875, Brigham Young University took its current name in 1903. The first doctoral program was offered in 1957, and course and degree offerings have continued to grow. The campus sits in the foothills of Provo, Utah, about 30 miles south of Salt Lake City. In 2006, *Princeton Review* named BYU the Best Value Private University. Students from BYU consistently compete competitively in every field. The campus now has more than 30,000 students from freshmen to postdoctoral. The library, one of the showpieces of campus, sits in the center of campus and is the central gathering location for study.

Information Commons Description

The Information Commons in the Harold B. Lee Library on the campus of Brigham Young University is an open space near the entrance of the library on the main (third) floor. The Commons consists of a single area with many types of study spaces: individual computer stations, collaboration computer stations (wired with extra power and network lines for laptop use), group study rooms with computer and projector, study tables (wired with extra power and network lines for laptop use), individual study carrels, soft chairs, and a multimedia lab for audio and video production. The space includes access to the campus wireless network. Many of the chairs in the Commons have wheels, allowing for easier configurability for group study. In addition, two partners share the space: the Publication Lab, where students can get help getting their work published, and the Writing Fellows, who provide assistance to students who need help with writing.

Services are provided in three locations by students and full-time librarians and staff with specific expertise: reference assistance, computer assistance, and multimedia assistance.

Reference assistance is offered at the desk by the entrance, along with directional information and referral to other parts of the Commons or the library. Reference services offered include traditional and electronic reference, including research using online databases. Reference desk staff are also able to answer some basic computer questions, especially when the computer assistant is busy. The nonstudent employees of the Commons teach first-year writing classes for Library Instruction. The student employees are trained for, and occasionally provide support to, those classes as instruction TAs.

The computer assistants and multimedia assistants are part of one core of students and staff. Each is able to work as either a computer assistant or multimedia assistant. Their training is done together and therefore they know all the same things. Computer assistants support all the computers in the Commons and are on call for computer-related issues that may come up in the rest of the library. There is also one computer assistant staffed in the periodicals section of the library during the busy hours of the day. Computer assistants are able to answer computer questions regarding all software installed on the computers. Often the computer assistant works with patrons, mostly students, in the Commons, creating the opportunity for reference students and staff to help answer questions the computer assistant would normally answer.

Multimedia assistants are required to know how to produce video and audio using both Windows and Mac operating systems. The Multimedia Lab holds two Windows and four Mac computers for multimedia production and two that have the Macromedia suite and other high-end production software. There are also two analog-to-digital duplication racks. These facilities are available to all who visit the Information Commons, including patrons from the community.

Information Commons Service Transaction Statistics

Statistics are kept on a sampling schedule in the entire library but not for the Commons specifically. Estimates based on those samples for 2005 by area served are as follows: computer/multimedia assistance 14,912; information desk 7,496; reference assistance 18,512, for a total of 40,920.

Information Commons Staffing and Training

The Information Commons is staffed all hours the library is open. Most positions in the Commons were created from personnel working in the General Reference department. The position of Information Commons section head was added after the Commons had been open for some months.

We have two full-time librarians, one 0.75 FTE librarian, two full-time staff, and approximately twenty student employees. One reference assistant and one multimedia/computer assistant are assigned to work during all times the library is open, 7:00 a.m. to midnight. During the hours of 8:00 a.m. to 6:00 p.m. there is an additional multimedia/computer assistant assigned to the Multimedia Lab, and between 9:00 a.m. and 4:00 p.m. an additional computer assistant is assigned to work in the periodicals section of the library. Full-time employees are available from 7:00 a.m. to 5:00 p.m., and one is assigned to the reference desk from 8:00 a.m. to 5:00 p.m. Monday through Friday and 6:00 p.m. to 10:00 p.m. Monday through Thursday.

Formal training takes place weekly in meetings held in a library instruction classroom. Informal training is ongoing and forms the foundation of weekly training topics. Training is meant to provide knowledge about current topics of interest for our patrons. We attempt to have our students prepared before the questions come.

What's on the Desktop

Most computers are based on the same campus-wide image, which includes word processing, spreadsheets, and class-specific software access. The computers in the Commons can be divided into five different software combinations, depending on function. Some have only access to a web browser and are not authenticated; these are for public or other use less than ten minutes and are

next to the reference desk. Most of the individual and collaboration stations contain the basic campus image and nothing more. The other individual and collaboration stations have, in addition to the image, a scanner and software for scanning. A few computers are dedicated to website and graphics creation and editing and contain the relevant software in addition to the image. Another group are the multimedia computers, which do not have the image installed but have the necessary software for editing audio and video. All computers can print to a central library queue that allows jobs to be sent to any printer in the building.

Information Commons Assessment

LibQUAL+, WOREP, and Project SAILS have recently been completed in the library. These provide an assessment of the library as a whole.

Statistics are kept on a sampling schedule at all reference desks, including in the Information Commons. The Commons statistics include questions asked of the computer and multimedia assistants. Recently a question arose about how the Commons is being used and whether it is being used by groups or individuals. Since June 2005, statistics have been kept on how many groups use the commons every hour. These statistics continue to be kept and analyzed. There are also plans to implement a more formalized assessment program in the Information Commons.

Information Commons Governance

The Information Commons at Brigham Young University is contained within the Public Services Division of the library. The Commons is managed by a librarian who has three full-time employees reporting to him. Each supervises different areas of responsibility within the Commons: desk reference assistance, online reference, and computer/multimedia assistance. The Information Commons section head reports to the General Information Services chair, who in turn reports to the assistant university librarian for public services.

Decisions regarding the Commons generally go from the bottom up. Library administrators understand that those working on the front lines are the ones who understand the needs and desires of patrons using the Commons. Major decisions or changes are approved first by the department chair and then, if necessary, by the assistant university librarian for public services. All changes and decisions are made with the mission and aims of the university and library in mind.

Lessons Learned

▌ Increasing the number of computers incrementally helped us determine the ideal number of computers for the area. We went through three different numbers and have finally found the one that keeps the lines to a minimum and still serves all types of studiers (i.e., groups and individuals at both computers and study tables).

▌ As much as we believe that everything for general library research has gone online, we do still have a few books that are used by the patrons. Our general reference collection has also gone through phases or phasing out. Books have also been moved to less prominent locations in the Information Commons.

▌ If there is new technology that will make the academic lives of our students better or easier, and if it is implemented and marketed well, it will be used. And the Information Commons is the ideal place to do the implementation. The multimedia section of the Commons has been a huge success and has and will continue to undergo incremental growth, in terms of both number of stations and space provided.

UNIVERSITY OF CALGARY

UNIVERSITY LIBRARY MACKIMMIE LIBRARY

Prepared June 2006 by Susan Beatty (Head, Information Commons, University of Calgary Library)

Library website	http://library.ucalgary.ca
IC website	http://library.ucalgary.ca/services/informationcommons/
Carnegie classification	Not applicable
# Undergraduates	23,071 FTE
# Graduate students	5,127 FTE
# Faculty	2,209
Highest degree offered	Doctorate
# Volumes	2,535,714
# Titles	1,644,207
# Periodical titles	353,872
# FTE librarians	43
# Other FTE staff	155 support, 22 casual
Library annual budget	$22,619,301
Annual circulation	349,609 initial loan, 1,294,321 renewals, 106,473 reserve loans
Annual gate entries	14,065 (single day, peak-period sample)
IC opening date	1999
IC name	Information Commons
IC service model type	Primarily integrated services
# Computer workstations	230 PCs
What's on desktop	Internet access, MS Office, specialized software, library research databases
IC architect	Chomik Architectural Group
Hours	24/5 Sun. 10:00 a.m.–Fri. 7:45 p.m., Sat. 10:00 a.m.–5:45 p.m. (fall and winter terms); reduced hours spring and summer
IC area	42,043 sq. ft.
# Physical service points in IC	3
Average # IC users in a typical month	Peak times 5,000 users per day
Print reference materials in the IC?	Yes

Location of Institution and Campus Description

The University of Calgary is a comprehensive university situated in a beautiful parklike setting in the northwest part of Calgary, Alberta. The university celebrated its fortieth anniversary in 2006. It is a 213-hectare campus housing sixteen faculties with fifty-three departments as well as more than thirty research institutes and centers. Included among the more than 26,000 students are some 900 international students from eighty-seven countries. The University of Calgary is one of Canada's top seven research universities.

Information Commons Description

The Information Commons is an integrated service facility that focuses on complete service to the user. Information Resources (IR) and Information Technologies (IT) collaborate to provide expert reference and technical assistance from one main service desk. The Information Commons is on the second floor of the University Library. In addition to the main service desk, which is the primary reference service point for the library, there is a service desk and seven PCs with specialized software for maps, academic data, and geographic information (MADGIC) and a service desk for document delivery service.

There are a total of 230 PCs in the Commons available to all users. Fifty of the computers are in a classroom, which can be divided into two twenty-five-seat classrooms. When the classroom area is not being used for information literacy or productivity software instruction, it is open to students. Because the library is a research center, it is open to all users; no authentication is required to use the computers. However, to print from the networked printers, the user must have a print card or student campus card to use as a debit card. Aside from the computers, there are twelve collaborative workrooms, three of which have PCs, all of which have Ethernet connections and two of which have DVD/VHS players and monitors. Workrooms are bookable online by campus members for one to two hours weekly.

A special media area has two scanners, six PCs, and specialized software products that are not available on the general download. The Commons also houses an adaptive technology workroom that is available only to students who are registered with the campus Disability Resource Centre; specialized software is recommended by the Centre.

The Information Commons has twenty-six laptop docking stations and also has wireless access.

Information Commons Service Transaction Statistics

On average over the past three years there have been more than 75,000 service transactions annually at the Information Commons. Half are reference transactions and half technical transactions.

Information Commons Staffing and Training

A mix of experts provide service in the Information Commons. Librarians and paraprofessionals provide reference service and information literacy instruction. Two IT specialists and sixteen student assistants provide expert technical instruction and one-on-one assistance. Rounding out the picture, two night assistants provide directional library assistance and technical assistance during the 24/5 overnight service hours.

Reference service is provided 66 hours per week and technical assistance is provided all hours the Commons is open. Evening, Saturday, and Sunday reference is available during fall and winter terms. Reference service is available on Saturdays during the spring term. There is no reference service available on weekends during the summer. MADGIC and document delivery desks are open more limited hours, Monday to Friday only.

Librarians and paraprofessionals work side by side with the IT staff from one integrated service desk.

Initial training for the IC staff included basic training on MS Office products for all library staff who would be working in the Commons. Student assistants and IT staff received an orientation to library service. Ongoing training for new IC staff includes orientation to the reference service, reference standards, and print and digital collections as well as the services offered in the Commons.

Annually as new student IT assistants are hired, they are introduced to library services, basic directional information, and policies and procedures. All of the documentation is posted on the student assistant Blackboard site, which also serves as a daily communication tool. This site is the students' knowledge base; they are expected to check and contribute to it on a daily basis. Technical updates as well as service policies and procedures, scheduling changes, and other announcements are posted on this site.

What's on the Desktop

All of the PCs in the Commons have the same download with Internet access, productivity software, and specialized research sources. The printing is networked and allows students to connect to any of the printers (five monochrome and one color). The special media area where the scanners reside has software such as Adobe Photoshop.

Information Commons Assessment

A user feedback form is posted on the Commons website. This has been a good tool for receiving immediate feedback and information on issues of the day as well as gauging longitudinal concerns about the service. The library has also participated in two LibQUAL+ surveys (2002 and 2004). Although the focus of the surveys was the users' perceptions of service quality on the library as a whole, good information was received regarding users' attitudes toward service, access, and place, which mentioned the Information Commons.

Information Commons Governance

The Information Commons is a collaborative service. The head of the Commons reports to the assistant director for Client Services, but other IR units as well as IT have interests in the operations, planning, and decision making regarding the services, policies, and procedures of the Commons. The head of the Commons chairs the Information Commons Operational team (ICOPS), which meets regularly to discuss issues and concerns on operations and to make decisions or recommendations as needed. The team is made up of representatives from Client Services, Liaison Services, Information Technology Services (IR), MADGIC, and Access Services; representatives from two branches that have small commons (Law and Health Sciences); and IT representatives—the manager of IT Client Services and the IT/Information Commons supervisor (supervisor of the IT student assistants).

There is no budget line in the IR budget other than for staffing: head, IC support staff of 5 FTE, part-time reference librarian (0.6 FTE), and night assistants (2 FTE/8 months). All other operational and capital costs are within the larger IR budget. Although IT and IR share the costs for the student IT assistants, IT pays for the IT staff in the Commons (2 FTE).

Lessons Learned

▌ Bring your partners together at the very beginning of your planning. Share your cultures so that you can begin to understand each other. Leadership in collaboration starts at the top. If you collaborate, the leaders of the various units need to be involved all the way through all phases—conception, implementation, and evolution—and they need to continue to communicate with each other and with their staff on the value of the collaboration.

▌ To produce the best service model you need to focus on user needs—not on what the various people at the table might think they themselves want for themselves or the user. Clarity of focus helps reduce conflict. You need to create a vision that is clear, concise, and relevant to the user as well as the service providers, and you need to continue to refer to the vision when you are making ongoing decisions.

▌ If you are successful, the students will think of the Commons as their space. Treat them with respect; listen to what they want. Keep the space open, warm, welcoming. Make sure that you have people working in the Commons who value the customer and know how to deliver good service.

CALIFORNIA POLYTECHNIC STATE UNIVERSITY, SAN LUIS OBISPO

ROBERT E. KENNEDY LIBRARY

Prepared June 2006 by Mary M. Somerville, Ph.D. (Assistant Dean, Information and Instructional Services, Robert E. Kennedy Library, and Convener, Learning Commons Partners) and David D. Gillette, Ph.D. (Associate Professor and Director, New Media Arts Program, College of Liberal Arts)

Library website	http://www.lib.calpoly.edu
IC website	http://learningcommons.lib.calpoly.edu
Carnegie classification	Master's Colleges and Universities (larger programs)
# Undergraduates	17,488
# Graduate students	987
# Faculty	1,246
Highest degree offered	Master's
# Volumes	755,568
# Periodical titles	7,029
# FTE librarians	13
# Other FTE staff	38
Library annual budget	$5,250,000 (includes IC)
Annual circulation	150,065
Annual gate entries	528,171
IC opening date	2005
IC name	Learning Commons
IC service model type	Primarily integrated services
# Computer workstations	80 Macs and PCs
What's on desktop	Internet browser, proprietary research databases, word processing, spreadsheet, desktop publishing, graphics, mathematics/statistics, multimedia, presentation
Hours	All hours the library is open: Mon.–Thurs. 7:00 a.m.–12:00 a.m.; Fri. 7:00 a.m.–5:00 p.m.; Sat. 10:00 a.m.–5:00 p.m.; Sun. 10:00 a.m.–12:00 a.m.
IC area	10,134 sq. ft.
# Physical service points in IC	1
Average # IC users in a typical month	2,500
Print reference materials in the IC?	No

Location of Institution and Campus Description

California Polytechnic State University ("Cal Poly") is a nationally ranked, four-year, comprehensive public university located in San Luis Obispo, California. The emphasis of the university is to create a "learn by doing" educational experience for its more than 18,000 students. With an emphasis on undergraduate study, Cal Poly prepares graduates for careers in applied technical and professional fields. Many students seek admission to Cal Poly not only because of its excellent academic reputation but also because the 6,000-acre main campus is nestled in the foothills of San Luis Obispo, just minutes from California's Central Coast beaches and nearby vineyards. Cal Poly is part of the twenty-three-campus California State University system, the nation's largest four-year university system.

Information Commons Description

The Cal Poly Learning Commons concept encourages students to become the center of their educational process. Unlike traditional methods of top-down, instructor-centered knowledge distribution, the Cal Poly Learning Commons is designed to help students discover and then refine their own methods for acquiring and putting to use the knowledge provided them as part of the university environment. Working together in the Learning Commons and adjacent facility spaces, librarians, instructional designers, pedagogy experts, and technologists support creative approaches to teaching and learning that seamlessly integrate technology with the construction of individual and shared knowledge.

PHASE ONE (AY 2004–2005)

Phase One activities involved planning for and building the infrastructure for virtual and face-to-face learning on the second floor of the university library. This collaborative remodeling activity involved faculty professional development and required campus information technologists and university library representatives to make decisions together. In the process, everyone involved in the development process created a shared vision for the physical and virtual spaces that would constitute the Learning Commons. In keeping with the university's "learn by doing" educational philosophy, the Commons partners made certain they used constructivist principles when designing systems and spaces to provide for student interaction. Appropriate to the polytechnic mission of the institution, the partners also agreed to emphasize information, communication, and technology proficiencies for lifelong learning. Because the partners worked with a shared sense of purpose, they were able to adapt many existing curricula and discipline-specific pedagogies to the new technology and information consultation services provided by the Learning Commons.

The evolving Cal Poly Digital Teaching and Learning Initiative (DTLI) ensures student success through faculty development activities that

promote instructional experimentation and curriculum renewal and transformation;

encourage faculty and staff to develop and demonstrate innovative approaches to teaching and learning that use technology and electronic information resources;

enable faculty, staff, and students to develop information, communication, and technology capabilities for successful learning in the Digital Age;

foster and disseminate research and scholarship that encourages the rigorous assessment and evaluation of technology and information-based teaching and learning.

The accomplishment of these Phase One outcomes required reorganizing some key library assets. We moved our information specialists and professional development experts into the same area, adjacent to the Learning Commons, thereby providing faculty with easy "one-stop" access. We also ensured that innovative pedagogy and technology development projects that could benefit a wide range of university faculty were also housed at the center of the Learning Commons environment. We refer to this physical as well as organization centering as the "innovation zone."

The first group of faculty and students to take up residence in the innovation zone was the Lumiere Ghosting Project, a new-media collaboration of faculty, students, and staff working to create a new form of interactive, fully immersive, Internet-enabled 3D cinema. The main curricular goal of this project is to integrate the technology invention process with a pedagogy focused on the history and theory related to modern media interconnection, distribution, and public use. The main production goal of the project is to create a Lumiere ghosting device—an interactive 3D cinema theater connected to other Lumiere ghosting devices (theaters) through a high-speed connection to the next generation of the Internet (Internet2). Participants in each Lumiere ghosting device around the world can see, talk to, and freely interact with each other through the use of full-scale 3D interactive puppets (avatars) that use images of the actual participants for the puppet face, body, hands, and feet. In each device all participants share the same virtual environment, which can be used for open collaboration, artistic expression, gaming, training, and interactive storytelling. By making use of recent developments in higher processing speeds, larger bandwidth capacities, and smaller computing and projection systems, the Lumiere ghosting device will be portable, so the entire device can be assembled, calibrated, connected to the Internet, and made completely operational in an afternoon by a technical crew of three or four people.

Allowing the Lumiere Ghosting Project to take up temporary residence in the Learning Commons has resulted in an effective blending and strengthening of the pedagogical and lifelong learning concerns of both collaborating Learning Commons partners and the Lumiere Ghosting Project team. The Learning Commons innovation zone has also provided a space and accompanying resources for the Lumiere Ghosting team (students and faculty) to begin developing full-scale demonstration versions of the ghosting device. In the short time the two organizations have been collaborating, a great deal has been achieved in promoting a constructivist learning process that strengthens four main elements of knowledge creation required for building effective and sustainable learning: intellectual application, social application, personal application, and practical application.

PHASE TWO (AY 2004–2006)

Concurrent with construction of the Phase One Commons, Cal Poly students have been invited to make recommendations for the student-centered Phase Two Commons. Under the supervision of faculty in human-computer interaction, human-information interaction, and technical communication, five courses have focused on investigating Cal Poly students' virtual and physical learning needs. Their recommendations include technology-enabled rooms for small group collaborative work and multimedia production facilities with ample social space to encourage serendipitous interdisciplinary exchanges. Several projects explored digital access strategies to the intellectual content of culminating senior projects, as well as "referral systems" to facilitate student identification of appropriate faculty sponsors. On the virtual domain, student-generated recommendations emanating from focus groups and usability studies on the library website informed a comprehensive information architecture redesign. In addition, library and information science, human-computer interaction, and knowledge management graduate students at Cal Poly and social informatics students at Luleå University of Technology in Sweden tested several digital learning and communication technologies and evaluated their efficacy for enabling Learning Commons virtual collaboration goals. These student-centered participatory design strategies provided Learning Commons partners with rich evidence from which to make planning decisions.

Information Commons Service Transaction Statistics

At present, Learning Commons transaction statistics are limited to hourly counts of workstation users and aggregated counts of Knowledge Station (public service desk) inquiries. Admittedly, these measures are inadequate to capture "what is really happening" in this collaborative space. See the assessment section below.

Information Commons Staffing and Training

With only an initial $250,000 "minor cap" investment and equipment from two former campus computer labs, the Learning Commons greatly depends on making effective use of existing staff shifted into remodeled facilities on the second floor of the library. In the initial startup year, one-time funds were received for employing student consultants at the Knowledge Station public service desk.

To ensure shared technical and research proficiency among student and staff employees, the Cal Poly training program borrowed heavily from the student navigation assistant training model developed in the University of Southern California Information Commons.

In addition, librarians work closely with academic faculty in the adjacent professional development facilities dedicated to hands-on curriculum transformation activities. No librarians staff the Knowledge Station service desk; rather, referrals are made to subject specialists on an as-needed basis.

Information Commons Assessment

Ongoing evaluation of the technical, resource, and service infrastructure of the Commons informs continuous improvements intended to close user expectation gaps identified in an Association of Research Libraries LibQUAL+ survey implemented in April 2004. Other evidence includes responses gathered from user surveys and focus groups, supplemented by user interviews and informal obser-

vations by the staff and instructors involved with the Learning Commons.

The more difficult-to-measure outcomes relate to assessment of faculty professional development and to student success in meeting course-related learning outcomes based on student interaction with the Learning Commons environment. Determination of methods to be used to assess faculty professional development is under discussion. At this time, the assessment of student success within the Commons environment is typically embedded within the courses currently meeting in the Commons. For example, in New Media Art I, Professor Gillette connected the curriculum of the course directly to development of the Lumiere ghosting device and then established performance-based methods for evaluating student comprehension of the media theory, history, and media development techniques that drive technology development for the project.

In a dedicated faculty development center located adjacent to the Learning Commons, a team of instructional designers, technology experts, and information specialists consult with faculty to help develop methods to develop student competencies. The Commons provides the laboratory for faculty members' experimental implementations.

Information Commons Governance

Decisions on concepts, policies, and procedures and oversight of operations are provided by the Learning Commons partners. Members represent Information Technology Services, the Robert E. Kennedy Library, and the Center for Teaching and Learning. In addition, the Academic Senate Instructional Advisory Committee on Computing and the Student Campus Computing Committee ensure faculty and student consultative advisement from all Cal Poly colleges.

Lessons Learned

▌ The location of a commons (physical and organizational) is vitally important in shaping how it is perceived and how it is used over time. When building a learning space designed to gather human and technological resources from all over a diverse campus, physically locating the organization at the "center" of the university is essential. Just as in commercial real estate practice, the location of a site determines to a great extent how it is perceived in the minds of those who encounter it and thereby also determines how visitors use the facility at that location. In many ways the library is physically central to much of Cal Poly's academic life, but for reasons that are not immediately apparent. We would like to say that students and faculty flock to the library to use the information resources available there, but instead students tend to use the library primarily as a convenient meeting and study space and the faculty therefore follow on this by working with their students on an informal basis there as well. The library is also near the central "green" for the campus and is at the nexus point on campus for the transportation system (roads, sidewalks, bus stops, parking lots, etc.); therefore, everyone on campus passes through the library plaza at least once a day.

▌ Even noble, supportive, and truly beneficial ideas are never exempt from considerations of politics and institutional "turf" disputes. (Politics are always local.) As we mentioned above, being centered in the library was ideal for the Learning Commons. In terms of politics, no one specifically "owns" the Commons, but at the same time it is available to everyone. Declaring independence from any particular department or college is important when starting a new interdisciplinary center or program of any kind. The less a new organization is associated with tangled and long-remembered political histories, the easier it is for that organization to try something new and to be launched into the public mind with a truly fresh beginning. However, being freed from old academic associations and their political connections also means that no one particular department, college, or program is immediately available to stand up

and protect the newly developed organization from financial or structural attack. Being free from previous associations also means being free from established and credited academic history, which can therefore lead to the impression that, since it's new it's trivial, and therefore simply an "extra" that can be easily discarded in dire financial times (which means being continually under attack since dire finances seems to be the continual financial state for most American state universities). Standing alone also means it's easy to be knocked down, or at the very least ignored. To help provide some cover, the library did declare primary ownership and protection for the Learning Commons, but because of its diversified mission for serving the university and a tendency toward conciliation the library as an organization was not always an ideally protective partner.

▌ Good and seemingly obvious ideas, centers, and organizations always need basic and devoted promotion to ensure they become visible in the public mind and to demonstrate continually their essential benefits to the world surrounding them. (If you build it, they don't always come.) The physical centering of the library makes it an ideal location for our Learning Commons, since it is in a building that is in use by nearly everyone on campus on a regular basis. Even though our library is not used in a traditional fashion (as an indexed repository of academic information used mainly for study and book-based research), as are fewer and fewer libraries, the library building is indeed at the center of much of Cal Poly life, with students continually using the building for meetings, informal browsing of the information resources available there, meeting with information specialists (librarians and other library staff), and as a collaboration and creation space (through extensive use of workrooms and computer labs). The faculty also see the library as a central part of their academic experience and often visit the building to use the printed resources and meeting facilities.

UNIVERSITY OF GEORGIA

STUDENT LEARNING CENTER

Prepared August 2006 by Florence King (Head, Student Learning Center and Associate University Librarian for Human Resources) and William G. Potter, Ph.D. (University Librarian and Associate Provost)

Library website	http://www.libs.uga.edu
IC website	http://www.slc.uga.edu
Carnegie classification	Research Universities (very high research activity)
# Undergraduates	25,002
# Graduate students	8,456
# Faculty	2,956 faculty (instruction/research/public services), 3,559 administrative/other professional
Highest degree offered	Doctorate
# Volumes	4,200,000
# Serial titles	48,000
# FTE librarians	70 for entire library, 6.5 for IC
# Other FTE staff	200 for entire library, 3 for IC
Library annual budget	$22,600,000 (no separate budget for IC operation)
Annual circulation	469,062 (FY2006)—includes circulation and physical reserves
Annual gate entries	922,437 for Main Library and Science Library, 1.8 million for IC (FY2006)
IC opening date	August 2003
IC name	Student Learning Center
IC service model type	Primarily integrated services
# Computer workstations	500 PCs
What's on desktop	Internet, proprietary research databases, office suites, word processing, spreadsheet, charting/graphing, desktop publishing, graphics, mathematics/statistics, multimedia/presentation
IC architect	Cooper Carry of Atlanta
Hours	Mon.–Thurs. 7:30 a.m.–2:00 a.m.; Fri. 7:30 a.m.–9:00 p.m.; Sat. 10:00 a.m.–7:00 p.m.
IC area	ca. 200,000 sq. ft. divided roughly in half: Electronic Library (2,240 seats) and classrooms (2,200 seats)
# Physical service points in IC	6
Average # IC users in a typical month	200,000 during fall/spring semesters
Print reference materials in the IC?	Yes, a small collection of ca. 60 titles.

Location of Institution and Campus Description

Chartered by the Georgia General Assembly in 1785, the University of Georgia is the nation's oldest state university and the birthplace of the American system of public higher education. The University of Georgia offers nineteen baccalaureate degrees in more than 150 fields, thirty master's degrees in 128 fields, twenty educational specialist degrees, three doctoral degrees in 90 areas, professional degrees in law, pharmacy, and veterinary medicine, and 139 Study Abroad and exchange programs.

The 2005 "Best Colleges" edition of *U.S. News & World Report* ranked UGA nineteenth among national public research universities. *Kiplinger's Magazine* ranked UGA sixth in its 2006 list of the "100 Best Values in Public Colleges." UGA boasts 500 registered student organizations, including thirty-two social fraternities and twenty-two social sororities.

The main campus comprises 380 buildings on 615 acres. Total system acreage, in thirty-four Georgia counties, is 42,247 acres. The University of Georgia's main campus is in Athens, Georgia (Clarke County), about 60 miles northeast of downtown Atlanta.

Information Commons Description

Half-classroom building and half-library, the Student Learning Center is designed to be an academic crossroads where students gather to take classes, consult electronic databases, study alone or in groups, write term papers, prepare classroom presentations, discuss a project with a professor over a cup of coffee, work with a team on a class project, or simply sit and read a book.

The Student Learning Center is an unusual approach to an information commons in that it is a separate building and integrates classroom and library space while providing abundant support from librarians, instructional technologists, computer specialists, and others. In a very short time, the Student Learning Center has become the center for teaching and learning for undergraduate students.

CLASSROOM SPACE

2,200 seats, supported by Center for Teaching and Learning and Enterprise Information Technology Services (campus computing center)

Twenty-six classrooms: three large lecture halls (280 seats), three medium lecture halls (140 seats), five small lecture halls (80 seats), ten medium classrooms (40 seats), five small classrooms (24 seats)

Advanced classroom technology controlled with instructor podium with wireless touch panel system for control of audiovisual source, video projector, audio level, lighting, screens, window shades: two projection screens, chalkboards, and whiteboards; video projector; laptop computer connection; laptop in the instructor's podium; VCR and DVD; cable TV tuner; high-resolution document camera; slide projector control; program audio sound system; auxiliary inputs to allow other audiovisual devices to be viewed and heard in the room (digital VCR player, portable videoconferencing cart); multiple audiovisual feeds; wireless microphones and voice amplification system for the large auditorium classrooms

Three faculty preparation rooms for use by instructors for class preparation

Center for Teaching and Learning classroom support offices and lab for technology training for faculty

LIBRARY SPACE

2,240 seats, supported by University Libraries and Enterprise Information Technology Services

500 computers for accessing the Web, 21,000 full-text journals and 29,000 full-text books, GALILEO research databases and electronic indexes, and a full range of word processing, spreadsheet, and other software packages

Professional research and computer use assistance via a reference desk, online chat, phone, and e-mail

Ninety-six group study rooms seating six to ten people that provide private areas for collaborative work, study sessions, preparation for presentations and projects, and breakout areas where faculty meet with smaller groups of students

Four state-of-the-art advanced learning labs dedicated to teaching electronic research and information literacy skills, faculty technology development, and software applications use (seating 16–38 students)

More than 2,400 laptop connections in a pervasive wireless network

Event spaces conducive to academic activities and functions (Fourth floor Rotunda and North Tower)

Traditional library furniture made of solid cherrywood

Comfortable study areas furnished with soft seating

Traditional reading room

24/7 access to portions of the building allowing use of computers and providing study space

Coffeehouse

Information Commons Service Transaction Statistics

Desk statistics. Of our approximately 21,000 questions at the service desks, 49 percent were directional or referral, 26 percent were machine maintenance, 19 percent were graphics, software, and wireless, and 6 percent were reference/research.

Laptop loan checkout statistics. We began loaning ten laptops in April 2006. April–June 2006 statistics: 460 laptop loan transactions.

Instruction statistics. Of 707 instruction sessions given by the University Libraries, 216 (31 percent) were taught by the librarians at the Student Learning Center.

Gate counts. Because there are almost twenty entrances and exits to the building, it is difficult to get a gate count in the traditional sense. Gate counters are placed on the most popular doors and in the elevator lobbies and staircases leading up from the first floor (which is all classroom). Also, we do an hourly count of the people in the building, which has been of great benefit in evaluating hours to be open, heaviest use areas of the building, and heaviest use hours in the building.

Information Commons Staffing and Training

The desks at the Student Learning Center are staffed most hours the building is open but not all. Enterprise Information Technology Services student consultants staff the desks all but ten hours the building is open; librarians staff the desk all but thirty-five of the 106 hours the building is open (mostly on weekends and late night). The six service desks are four desks manned by computing consultants (usually double staffed), one desk with computing consultant and librarian, and one desk with two security assistants who also provide information and direction. Another service point in the building (not mentioned in the tabular count) is the Classroom Support Office, out of which problem solving, maintenance, and training of faculty and students in the classroom technology come.

When the building opened, several new librarians and staff were hired for Libraries Reference as well as for building management and security. This met our minimal staffing needs for the building. In addition to the six librarians and one library staff who man the desk, reference librarians from the other libraries schedule a few hours on the Learning Center reference desk. As well, Learning Center librarians schedule two to four hours per week either at Main Library or Science Library to maintain their skills and interact with their reference colleagues in the other buildings. All staff in the Center's Electronic Library wear a badge that identifies them as reference librarians, but not by name. We find this essential in such a large space when the staff are frequently on the floor helping patrons.

Training, both primary and ongoing, is essential. The Student Learning Center librarians are involved with the training of the new student computing consultants and have developed tutorials and teaching modules to familiarize the students with the essential components of identifying databases, beginning searches, and composing search strategies. In-depth reference questions are referred to the reference desk librarian or an appointment is scheduled for a consultation. The Student Learning Center computing managers are the librarians in modules intended to enhance knowledge of software, technical expertise, and technical troubleshooting tips. Formal sessions are scheduled; as well, all staff share their knowledge to supplement their colleagues' lacks.

In addition to training in resources and software, it is also important that all staff remain current on more operational procedures in the building. Since there is not a traditional circulation area or administrative area to which patrons can be referred, the desk staff must know how to address everything from "how do I put money on my card?" to "I want to check out a laptop," to "hours," to "how do I schedule a classroom?" to "I need to find an empty group study room." A blog has been developed to share these kinds of changes with all staff.

What's on the Desktop

We offer a full range of software on each of the 500 PC workstations:

> Microsoft Windows
>
> Microsoft Office 2002 (XP Professional)
>
> Microsoft Internet Explorer
>
> Plug-ins: Macromedia Shockwave, Flash, Apple Quicktime, Chemscape Chime, Mathplayer, Deja-Vu
>
> Adobe Acrobat Reader
>
> J-edit and J-exam
>
> F-Secure Anti-Virus v. 5.3/Management Agent v. 4.50

> UGA Internet Kit: SSH Secure Shell, SSH File transfer, Secure TN3270
>
> Windows Media Player and Real One—Real Players
>
> Virtual Interactive Partner from Convey
>
> Free players and client browser plug-ins
>
> CD burner software

Additional software loaded on the twenty multimedia machines:

> Macromedia Fireworks and Dreamweaver
>
> Adobe Photoshop, Illustrator, and Go Live

Information Commons Assessment

SLC survey. Every spring since 2004, we have conducted a survey and follow-up focus groups that measured the use of the building, gathered demographic information, and then asked students to comment on how they use the building and its resources as well as on areas of concern or suggestions. We plan to continue these spring assessments so that we will have several years of similar data to measure.

Observational and anecdotal assessment. Because we are such a new facility, we rely heavily on suggestions made at the service desks, informal comments made in the hallways, our own student assistants (which number approximately sixty), and, of course, many discussions of our own about how things are (or are not) working optimally. We have been the topic of many cartoons and opinion pieces in the student newspaper, and we took these seriously, answering the opinion pieces when appropriate and learning from the cartoons which issues seemed to be big ones for students. For example, when we first opened, printing was a tough issue; we knew it, of course, but realized the extent that it was affecting the students when a cartoon was printed about it.

Suggestion box. We have an online e-mail suggestion box that students have used to send complaints and suggestions. We answer each one and then try and determine if that suggestion reflects minority or majority opinion. We will incorporate a physical suggestion box this fall and post the answers in a high-traffic area.

LibQUAL+. Our first participation in LibQUAL+ was in spring 2004. Although there were not specific questions about the Student Learning Center, there were many positive comments made about the facility. Our second LibQUAL+ survey was issued in spring 2007, and we gathered additional useful information about our services.

Gate counts and patron counts. As mentioned in the statistics section above, we use these to monitor use to help with staffing and security.

Information Commons Governance

The building is managed by a partnership of staff from three main campus departments: the University Libraries, Enterprise Information Technology Services (the campus computing area), and Center for Teaching and Learning (the faculty development and classroom support arm that reports to the vice president for instruction).

There is no single budget or administrative leader for the building. Areas of responsibility have been clearly laid out, and areas that cross over or are particularly challenging are worked out satisfactorily as they arise. We meet both formally and informally to maintain communication and to sort out new programs, services, or issues as they arise. Communication is key.

With the goal of the building to offer integrated resources and services, care was taken to involve faculty, students, staff, and administrators from many areas around campus in the facilities design and operations development of the building. During the planning process, committees comprising the president for instruction, vice president for student affairs, university librarian, chief information officer, and director of the Center for Teaching and Learning met regularly to develop overarching mission and goals for the building. A

more detailed operations and policy setting group, the SLC Support Partnership, comprising senior level staff from those same areas, began work on specific working policies for the facility. This group has continued to meet as needed since the building opened in August 2003 to develop new policies, discuss areas of concern, solve problems, and expand programs and services as needed. Specific information is available at http://www.libs.uga.edu/slc/planners.html.

Lessons Learned

▌ The reference librarian role has changed to a role more in line with the tasks of teaching, digital design, and public relations. Students and faculty do not always make the connection that this space is a library. This affects how they use the reference services, particularly the reference librarians, for help with research.

▌ It is imperative that all those involved with the administration of the space and programs embrace *flexibility* in their assumptions of how the space should be used, in policymaking, even in assumptions about "what a library is," down to the smallest details such as what color markers to provide for the whiteboards in the group study rooms, service desk location, vending machine placement, or provision of staplers. Be prepared to change policies (sometimes many times), be open to how the students and faculty want and need to use the space, and revamp accordingly.

▌ An administrative partnership of distinct groups can work and even strengthen the administration. Group management is possible when each member understands its role and is willing to chip in where needed. Acknowledgment that each member of the partnership has important insights and areas of expertise to bring to the project is key.

UNIVERSITY OF GUELPH

MCLAUGHLIN LIBRARY

Prepared June 2006 by Janet Kaufman (Head, Information Services and Co-Director) and
Nancy Schmidt, Ph.D. (Acting Associate Chief Librarian and Co-Director, Learning Commons)

Library website	http://www.lib.uoguelph.ca
IC website	http://www.learningcommons.uoguelph.ca
Carnegie classification	Not applicable
# Undergraduates	16,561
# Graduate students	2,055
# Faculty	776
Highest degree offered	Doctorate
# Volumes	1,559,078 including materials in off-site storage, not including microform
# Titles	1,173,811
# Periodical titles	15,877
# FTE librarians	28
# Other FTE staff	103
Library annual budget	C$13.8 million; IC funded by Library and Student Affairs with no separate budget
Annual circulation	436,825 in FY2004/2005
Annual gate entries	1.85 million
IC opening date	1999
IC name	Learning Commons
IC service model type	Somewhat integrated services
# Computer workstations	300 PCs; 100 laptops with wireless cards
What's on desktop	Internet, proprietary research databases, office suites, word processing, spreadsheet, charting/graphing, mathematics/statistics
IC architect	Not applicable; McLaughlin Library opened in 1968; project architect was L. S. Langmead of Hancock, Little, Calvert Associates
Hours	All hours the library is open: 7:00 a.m.–2:00 a.m. daily, Sept.–April; Mon.–Fri. 7:00 a.m.–10:00 p.m., noon–10:00 p.m., weekends and holidays, May–Aug.
IC area	26,605 sq. ft.
# Physical service points in IC	3
Average # IC users in a typical month	8,425 (74,503 user contacts/8 months of academic year)
Print reference materials in the IC?	No

Location of Institution and Campus Description

The University of Guelph was established in 1964 and is located in southwestern Ontario, Canada. The university has a unique atmosphere that goes back to its traditional roots in practical, innovative, and integrated learning. This is the legacy of the three founding colleges: Ontario Agricultural College (est. 1874), Ontario Veterinary College (est. 1862), and MacDonald Institute (est. 1903). The University of Guelph has a distinctive educational philosophy that is both learner centered and research intensive and emphasizes a collaborative approach to learning.

More than 16,600 undergraduate and graduate students in six colleges are enrolled in programs that span the arts, humanities, physical and natural sciences, and social sciences. These core disciplines are supplemented by interdisciplinary programs, a selected range of professional and applied programs, and areas of special responsibility in agri-food and veterinary medicine.

In addition to a 1,017-acre campus in Guelph, including a 408-acre arboretum and a 30-acre research park, the university has three regional campuses that offer diplomas in agriculture and applied training, outreach, and research to the agricultural community.

The university also has partnered with Humber Institute of Technology and Advanced Learning in Toronto to offer specialized programs that provide both a University of Guelph honors degree and a college diploma in four years of study. Currently, the University of Guelph–Humber offers six undergraduate diploma-degree programs in purpose-built facilities in the Greater Toronto area at Humber's north campus with more than 1,500 enrolled students.

Guelph is the second-most research-intensive university in Canada (based on the ratio of research funds to operating funds) and the first among non-medical schools, and it is currently building a science complex with almost 400,000 square feet of labs for research and teaching, offices, and meeting rooms. Guelph's first-year retention rate is above 90 percent and its graduation rate is 89 percent.

Information Commons Description

The Learning Commons at the University of Guelph brings together services in support of learning, writing, research, and use of technology. It is based on a partnership model with Learning and Writing Services from Student Affairs and the Library and Computing and Communications Services from Academic Affairs. This partnership model allows us to offer students a more coherent and integrated approach to academic support services and to apply the combined expertise of librarians, professional staff, and student peer helpers to meet students' diverse learning needs.

We have a mission statement that identifies our purpose and mandate and a set of guiding principles that reflect the shared commitment the partners bring to this collaborative environment. The Learning Commons has been intentionally located on the first floor of the McLaughlin Library in recognition of its role as a central gathering place for students to study, engage in writing and research, and learn in collaborative settings.

The Learning Commons offers services designed around four key pillars: learning, writing, research, and technology. We offer individual assistance, drop-in help, small and large group workshops, in-class presentations, supported study group sessions, and print and web-based resources. The services in the Commons include the following:

The *Information Technology Help Desk* is a service provided by Computing and Communications Services and is staffed by student consultants. It provides walk-up computing support for e-mail, software downloads, MS Office applications, scanning, and web publishing. Workshops are also available to help students make the most of campus information technology resources.

Learning Services provides programs and resources to enhance learning, academic performance, and self-management skills of undergraduate and graduate students. This service addresses specific learning topics such as learning from lectures, exam preparation, improving concentration, critical reading, effective group work, presentation skills, time management, and dealing with procrastination. Staff members also work with faculty and TAs on learning-related issues or design special services tailored to their students' specific needs.

The *Library Centre for Students with Disabilities* offers services and adaptive software that enable students with disabilities to access information resources in the library. Specialized equipment includes computers with adjustable-height worktables; accessible printing station; color, closed-circuit television; and desk-mounted and portable illuminated magnifying glass.

Research Help and Information Literacy. The library provides information, strategic research assistance, and consultations, referral, and instructional sessions. Research help is available in person or by e-mail, phone, or online chat. Librarians work closely with faculty to develop course-related and course-integrated instruction. Content may range from general library research skills to subject-specific information resources for assignments.

Supported Learning Group Program sessions (based on the Supplemental Instruction model) are student peer-facilitated group study sessions that enrich the learning experience of students enrolled in historically challenging first- and second-year courses. Sessions are regularly scheduled, informal opportunities for students to compare and process the quality and content of their notes, discuss readings, practice problem-solving strategies, and integrate study skills with course content.

Writing and ESL Services. Writing assistance is available to students who wish to enhance their writing skills as well as those who are faced with writing in a new genre, have difficulty writing critically and analytically, or whose first language is not English. Writing and ESL Services focuses on such topics as referencing; writing lab reports, literature reviews, and book reports; writing within specific disciplines; writing theses and dissertations; and ESL writing and communication support. In addi-

tion, this service group provides support to faculty and TAs in the use of writing in their courses.

Under our collaborative model, the Learning Commons is positioned to take on projects with broad institutional implications that are not easily claimed by either the library or Student Affairs or any single department. These collaborative ventures include academic integrity initiatives, involvement in writing in the disciplines, cosponsorship of the Teaching and Learning Innovations annual conference, development of the Graduate Student Learning Initiative, and the Reading Project.

Information Commons Service Transaction Statistics

The number of service transactions or users at the various public service desks in the Learning Commons is recorded, with the exception of the IT Help Desk. There are a total of almost 75,000 user contacts per year at the other service desks.

Information Commons Staffing and Training

No new positions were created to staff the Learning Commons; rather, staff and services were brought together in a single location.

Service desk hours in the Commons vary and are not staffed at all hours the library is open to the public. The Research Help Desk is open 9:00 a.m.–9:00 p.m. Monday–Thursday, 9:00 a.m.–4:30 p.m. Friday, and 1:00–4:30 p.m. on weekends and holidays. It is staffed by a mix of librarians and support staff. Research help staff rove to provide assistance. The IT Help Desk is staffed by hourly paid student employees hired by the Computing and Communications Services department. Learning and writing programs and services are provided by 7.5 FTE professional staff and eighty peer helpers who each work ten hours per week during the fall and winter semesters.

Training is specific to each service and is the responsibility of the associated managers. Peer helpers participate in a two-day training program before the semester begins and in regular training throughout the semester. IT student consultants also participate in regular training throughout the semester.

What's on the Desktop

All computers and laptops in the library have a common suite of software applications. They allow access to productivity software (e.g., office suites, spreadsheet, word processing/text editing, charting/graphing) and to the Internet and the library's proprietary research databases. Productivity software is provided through site licenses. Deep Freeze software ensures that software downloaded or installed by users is deleted when a workstation is rebooted. Networked printing is available at four print release stations and requires payment with a copy card. One color printer is available. Wireless printing is available from the library's laptops.

Information Commons Assessment

The members of the Learning Commons operational management group are committed to regular and systematic qualitative and quantitative assessment practices. All are responsible for ensuring that their programs and services are assessed regularly based on the practices, standards, and accountabilities unique to their respective professions. The variety of assessment measures used include workshop and in-class evaluations, comment cards, focus groups, session participation rates, grade performance measures, survey data, and end-of-semester qualitative feedback. As well, the partners collect their own statistics on usage counts, web hits, and number of students attending sessions, participating in workshops, and receiving individual assistance.

In 2003 the partners collaborated on a user needs survey to better understand the learning, writing, research, and technology needs of students at the undergraduate and graduate levels. The results were used to guide space renovation initiatives and identify areas for possible program expansion. Focus groups were used in the develop-

ment of an online survey sent to a random group of undergraduate and graduate students. Results of the survey indicated very strong support for extended building hours, access to laptop computers, a wireless network in the library, and the need for designated space for quiet study, group learning, and computing. As a result, hours were extended from the previous 8:30 a.m.–12:00 a.m. to 7:00 a.m.–2:00 a.m. daily from September to April; the laptop loan program was launched; and the library became a wireless environment in 2003. As well, the notion of "zoned space" was integrated into space renovations, completed in August 2005, which resulted in defined computing locations, casual seating areas, and group study spaces. Other survey results more specific to the actual services provided have been used for both short- and long-term planning and setting of priorities.

In fall 2004 the codirectors initiated discussions with the operational management group to develop expertise and understanding of assessment techniques, survey software, and the development of web-based surveys. This resulted in the piloting of an online satisfaction survey completed in winter 2005.

The LibQUAL+ instrument has provided formal assessment for library as a whole. The LibQUAL+ assessment was conducted in 2003 and again in 2005. LibQUAL+ defined and measured library service quality by surveying library users' perceptions of service quality, identifying gaps between desired, perceived, and minimum expectations of service. The library plans to administer the Project SAILS instrument to assess the information literacy skills of Guelph students; the timing is not yet determined. In addition, desk statistics are taken, reviewed, and discussed on a regular basis, and informal feedback from library users (e.g., from our question-and-answer board) is reviewed.

On the basis of feedback provided through specific program evaluations, comments, focus groups, and end-of-semester reports, student reaction to the Learning Commons has been overwhelmingly positive. From a usage perspective, there has been an increase in students attending workshops, participating in drop-in sessions, and receiving individual consultations every year since the Learning Commons was initiated in 1999.

The themes that continue to emerge in students' comments about the Learning Commons are the relevance of programs that help them to succeed and the opportunity to find such services in one location.

Information Commons Governance

The day-to-day management of the Learning Commons is the responsibility of two codirectors, who are responsible for providing leadership in developing and initiating collaborative opportunities among the partners. One oversees Learning Services, the Supported Learning Group Program, and Writing and ESL Services and reports to Student Affairs. The other is responsible for Reference and Information Literacy and the Library Centre for Students with Disabilities and is accountable to the library. Programming, budget, and staff responsibilities are specific to each director's area of operation.

A steering committee is chaired by the associate vice president (academic) and the associate vice president (student affairs) and includes the chief librarian/chief information officer, the director of teaching support services, and the two codirectors. This group sets policy and strategic direction for the Learning Commons.

An operational management group comprising senior staff professionals and librarians from each of the codirectors' areas meets regularly to identify and recommend needs for space and equipment; opportunities for collaboration, staff training, and development; solutions to problems; new or additional resources; and program and service priorities. Members of the operational management group provide regular updates on the programs for which they are responsible and report on emerging trends and patterns. They also undertake joint planning to ensure that programs are integrated whenever feasible.

Lessons Learned

▌ Programs and services are more important than space.

▌ Successful collaboration and partnership require commitment and an investment of time and energy. Sharing the vision of an information commons among the various partners is not the same as agreeing about how things should get done or even what should get done—this is where time and energy are needed.

▌ The library must be recognized to be both a social place and a study place.

▌ We have made changes to our space over several years as funds were available. This process of incremental change has been beneficial in that it allows us to try something and then make adjustments based on the results.

INDIANA UNIVERSITY BLOOMINGTON

HERMAN B WELLS LIBRARY

Prepared June 2006 by Diane K. Dallis (Head, Information Commons, Undergraduate Library Services) and Carolyn Walters (Executive Associate Dean of the IUB Libraries)

Library website	http://www.libraries.iub.edu
IC website	http://www.library.uncc.edu/ic/
Carnegie classification	Research Universities (very high research activity)
# Undergraduates	29,562
# Graduate students	7,442
# Faculty	1,865 full-time, 309 part-time
Highest degree offered	Doctorate
# Volumes	6,541,543
# Titles	4,586,894
# Periodical titles	61,386
# FTE librarians	84 for entire library, 6 for IC
# Other FTE staff	225 for entire library, 2 for IC
Library annual budget	$28,000,000
Annual circulation	652,715 (1,241,950 including renewals)
Annual gate entries	4,063,133
IC opening date	2003
IC name	Information Commons
IC service model type	Somewhat integrated services
# Computer workstations	330 PCs and Macintoshes
What's on desktop	Internet, subscription databases, word processing, spreadsheet, charting/graphing, desktop publishing, graphics, mathematics/ statistics, multimedia/presentation
IC architect	Veazey, Parrot, Durkin, and Shoulders
Hours	24 hours
IC area	35,000 sq. ft.
# Physical service points in IC	3
Average # IC users in a typical month	190,000
Print reference materials in the IC?	Yes, the reference collection for the Undergraduate Core Collection.

Location of Institution and Campus Description

Indiana University has eight campuses and was founded on the Bloomington campus in 1820. Fall 2005 enrollment at IU Bloomington was 29,562 undergraduate students and 7,442 graduate students. The student-faculty ratio is 18 to 1. There are 1,865 full-time faculty, 309 part-time faculty, 286 professional administrative personnel, and 5,129 full-time staff.

The Herman B Wells Library, with its twin towers of Indiana limestone, is the visual center of the library system and primarily supports the disciplines of the humanities and social sciences. More than 4.6 million volumes are held in this building. Especially noteworthy are the collections that support IU's international and area studies, including interdisciplinary research collections developed in the areas of African studies, Russian and East European studies, Uralic and Altaic studies, East Asian studies, and West European studies. The IU Bloomington libraries rank twelfth among member libraries of the Association of Research Libraries.

A team of specialists selects, manages, and builds our research collections, which include more than 6.6 million books in some 900 languages. The materials support every academic discipline on campus, with an emphasis on the humanities and social sciences. Collections also include journals, maps, films, and sound recordings. Users can access more than 400 databases, 43,000 electronic journals, and 224,000 electronic books as well as locally developed digital content.

All IU libraries are open to residents of the state as well as to IU faculty and students. Library staff members are available to assist users in locating materials and to teach effective methods of information use.

Information Commons Description

As a partnership between the IU Bloomington Libraries and University Information Technology Services, the Information Commons supports and enhances student learning and research by provid-ing state-of-the-art technology and resources in an academic environment. The Commons is located on the first two floors of the west tower of the Herman B Wells Library, which opened in 1969. It is a place for students to interact, get technology support and research assistance, attend technology and research workshops or classes, and work in groups or individually on course assignments. Each floor provides a distinct learning environment to accommodate the diverse learning styles and needs of IU Bloomington students: the 27,000-square-foot Information Commons 1, on the first floor of the west tower, opened in August 2003 and provides an environment conducive to active learning and collaborative work; the 8,000-square-foot Information Commons 2, on the second floor of the west tower, opened in March 2005 and provides an environment for quiet, individual work.

Information Commons Service Transaction Statistics

The west tower of the Herman B Wells Library received 1,703,125 visitors, and the 330 public workstations in the Information Commons were logged into 747,745 times during the 2004/2005 fiscal year. The following are Commons service transaction highlights for the year:

- Library reference interactions: 19,012
- Library instruction sessions: 403
- IT consultant contacts: 44,724
- IT Support Center walk-in contacts: 26,252
- IT Support Center carry-in contacts (work-stations dropped off to be fixed): 1,287
- Technology workshops classes: 235
- Undergraduate Core Collection circulation and in-house use: 27,513

Information Commons Staffing and Training

The Information Commons offers three combined service desks. The Library Customer and Access

Services Department (CASD) and the University Information Technology Services (UITS) Support Center share the desk at the main entrance to the Commons. The IC Undergraduate Library Services (ICUGLS) Department and the Student Technology Centers (STC) share the other two Commons service desks.

INFORMATION COMMONS 1 REFERENCE AND TECHNOLOGY CONSULTING DESK

Library reference services and STC consulting share a large service desk in the center of the first floor of the Commons. Librarians, support staff, and School of Library and Information Science graduate student employees of ICUGLS provide reference services for 101 of the 168 hours Information Commons 1 (IC1) is open each week. Library staff handle just over 19,000 reference interactions each year. There is typically one librarian and a library staff person or graduate student employee on duty during reference hours. Upper-level undergraduate student employees of the STC provide support 24 hours a day for the more than 180 software applications on the Commons workstations. There are typically one student shift supervisor and one to four technology consultants who handle more than 37,000 interactions a year. The technology consultants are hired on the basis of customer service experience and receive resource-based training. ICUGLS librarians participate in orientation/training for STC new hires. In addition, ICUGLS and STC hold team-building meetings once or twice per semester.

LIBRARY CIRCULATION AND IT SUPPORT CENTER DESK

Library circulation services and IT account and hardware support are located at a service counter at the entrance to IC1. Undergraduate student employees (from Customer and Access Services Department) provide circulation services 121 hours each week. Full-time staff and part-time student employees from the UITS Support Center offer walk-in help with IT accounts and repair personal computers and laptops for student, faculty, and staff for a fee. Support Center services are offered 92 hours per week. There is no cross-training and no interdepartmental meetings between these two units. The Libraries and UITS share the cost of hourly support for part-time security guards who work from midnight to 8:00 a.m. every day, except the five days each year the Information Commons is closed.

INFORMATION COMMONS 2 INFORMATION AND TECHNOLOGY SUPPORT

Directional assistance and technology support are offered at the service desk in Information Commons 2 (IC2), which is open 117 hours per week (2:00 a.m. Sunday–Thursday and midnight on Friday and Saturday). ICUS undergraduate student employees staff the desk 58 hours per week and provide assistance to library users in locating call numbers for the Core Collection, answering basic directional questions, and shelving and shelf-reading the Core Collection. The STC undergraduate students staff the IC2 desk all hours it is open and provide software support for the sixty-eight fixed workstations and students using the ninety data jacks and wireless connectivity for their laptops. Both units enforce the quiet and other Commons policies.

What's on the Desktop

The UITS Student Technology Center provides the IC hardware and delivers the 180 software applications to the desktop. Microsoft Office, Adobe software, and a variety of specialized departmental software packages are available. All workstations are on a three-year replacement cycle. The majority of the 330 workstations are Dell PCs, but 10 percent are Macintosh computers. The maintenance of the workstations is collaboratively managed by UITS and the Libraries. Group work is permitted only in IC1 (first floor), where forty-seven group workstations are located.

There are twenty-four workstations for multimedia work equipped with eleven scanners, microphones, various media readers, and CD and DVD burners. These workstations allow students to digitize video from VHS, mini-DV, or camcorder; digitize analog audio from cassette tape; edit video and analog; export digital audio and video to tape; and scan images and text.

Each IU Bloomington student is allotted a print quota of 650 monochrome pages per semester. Fees are charged and billed directly to the student for special printing. The printing is managed with Pharos Uniprint, and printers—nine monochrome laser (40 percent of total STC campus output), three color laser, two widebed plotters, and two inkjet miniplotters—are on a four-year replacement cycle.

Information Commons Assessment

Library and UITS partners work together to develop and conduct an IC user survey. Online surveys are conducted once each semester and the responses are reviewed and responded to by the Commons partner units. The UCUGLS department is currently planning to expand assessment activities to include regularly scheduled user or customer questionnaires to assess the quality of services and student experience. The current plan is to conduct three questionnaire exercises each semester.

Information Commons Governance

During planning for the Information Commons, the Library and UITS partners developed a memorandum of agreement describing the partnership and the terms for the operation of the facility. The agreement also defines the members of the governance group that guide the operation, advise on changes, and plan for the future growth of the Commons. The governance group comprises Libraries and UITS administrators and managers. Though not specifically stated in any document, the IC partners share

a strong commitment to student services. Both parties value the other's expertise and believe that the integration of services has benefited students. UITS and the Libraries are flexible and willing to adapt procedures and workflow as needed.

During the third year of operation, the Libraries and UITS developed a new group to oversee daily operations. The IC operations group comprises Libraries and IT managers who meet monthly to discuss ideas for changes, plan for assessment, and ensure the provision of excellent services. The group was formed in response to the need for managers and staff who participate in or oversee the daily services and resources to meet and communicate regularly. The operations group reports to the governance group and makes recommendations such as policy changes and facilities issues.

Lessons Learned

▌ Plan for the new staff culture that will and should develop among the frontline staff. The collaborative spirit among most of the IC partners at IU Bloomington is the most significant factor in the success of the Information Commons. The Libraries and the Academic Information Technology department should have a system or an organizational structure in place to nurture their relationship over time and through staffing changes.

▌ Develop a strong and clear memorandum of agreement with IC partners to help clarify all the resources, services, and responsibilities each partner brings to the Information Commons. As the IU Bloomington Libraries continue to expand their partnerships with other campus units, the memorandum has proved to be an excellent planning tool and a document that guides the relationships.

UNIVERSITY OF MASSACHUSETTS AMHERST

W. E. B. DU BOIS LIBRARY LEARNING COMMONS

Prepared June 2006 by Anne C. Moore, Ph.D. (Associate Director, User Services)

Library website	http://www.library.umass.edu
IC website	http://www.umass.edu/learningcommons/
Carnegie classification	Research Universities (very high research activity)
# Undergraduates	20,392
# Graduate students	4,254
# Faculty	1,147
Highest degree offered	Doctorate
# Volumes	3,204,025
# Periodical titles	41,308
# FTE librarians	55
# Other FTE staff	75 (does not include 46 FTE student assistants)
Library annual budget	$14,113,346 (FY2006) for library (plus $410,000 ongoing base budget for IC)
Annual circulation	408,867 (includes Integrated Sciences and Engineering Library and Music Reserve Lab in other buildings)
Annual gate entries	726,000
IC opening date	October 21, 2005
IC name	UMass Amherst Learning Commons
IC service model type	Primarily integrated services
# Computer workstations	58 library public PCs; 122 authenticated (106 PCs and 16 Macs); 17 Gateway M280 tablet PCs
What's on desktop	Browsers, Microsoft Office, licensed software of all types, including graphics, multimedia, statistical, and GIS programs
IC architect	Not applicable; floor plan/furnishings: OFI Contract Interiors, Springfield, Mass.
Hours	During academic semesters, the entire building is open: 11:00 a.m. Sun.–9:00 p.m. Fri.; 9:00 a.m.–9:00 p.m. Sat. (142 hours per week).
IC area	23,500 sq. ft. (renovated space)
# Physical service points in IC	4 on floor (plus 1 on the fly); 5 on other floors
Average # IC users in a typical month	60,000
Print reference materials in the IC?	Yes, the main print reference collection for the library (18,000 volumes).

Based on ARL 2004/2005 statistics unless otherwise noted.

Location of Institution and Campus Description

The University of Massachusetts Amherst was established in 1867 as a land grant agricultural college set on 310 rural acres, with four faculty members, four wooden buildings, fifty-six students, and a curriculum that combined modern farming, science, technical courses, and liberal arts.

The flagship campus of the commonwealth's university system, UMass Amherst is a major research university enrolling approximately 25,000 students from all fifty states and more than one hundred countries. Its ten schools and colleges offer eighty-seven undergraduate majors, seventy-three master's, and fifty-one doctoral programs. Sponsored research activities total more than $134 million a year.

A leading center for public higher education in the Northeast, UMass Amherst has gained a reputation for excellence in a growing number of fields, for its wide and varied academic offerings, and for its expanding historic roles in education, research, and public service.

Located on 1,450 acres in the scenic Pioneer Valley of western Massachusetts, the campus provides a rich cultural environment in a rural setting close to major urban centers. As a member of the Five College Consortium, UMass Amherst shares a mutually rewarding relationship with students from Amherst, Hampshire, Mount Holyoke, and Smith Colleges.

Information Commons Description

The UMass Amherst Learning Commons permeates the twenty-six-floor W. E. B. Du Bois Library, named the "tallest library in the world" upon its completion in 1973. Space (23,500 of 70,000 square feet) on the lower level, or footprint, of the building was renovated in a brief, four-month burst between May and September 2005 to form the "test bed" of a larger renovation for the building to meet the needs of twenty-first-century students. The new space wraps around an outdoor courtyard called the Oswald Tippo Library Courtyard Sculpture Garden (the Courtyard), with beautiful seasonal flowers tended by the library staff group called the "Deadheaders." In addition to the natural light, the lower level benefits from a campuswide lighting project, which transformed the formerly dark space into a vibrant area. Paint and flooring to complement the Herman Miller Resolve and Ethospace furnishings along with Caper chairs created the most popular hangout on campus for students of all majors and backgrounds to socialize, collaborate, and interact with library, technology, and academic support services. The new installation is flexible to adapt to the changing needs of students using the space and completely movable as additional renovations are planned and executed.

Exterior renovations have included new public spaces and plantings as well as a garden at the north end of the building presented by the class of 1955 alumni. Additional renovations and repairs to the HVAC, electrical, and interior of the lower level are planned for the next several years. These changes should allow for the shift of library staff housed on the lower level in a windowless area to share the natural light of the Courtyard with users and allow the Learning Commons to expand. In the future, furnishings complementary to those in the Learning Commons will be installed in the second-floor quiet study area. This area will have comfortable seating, individual study carrels, and additional workstations with state-of-the-art software for those who prefer quiet over the noisy, collaborative lower level.

Upon entering the W. E. B. Du Bois Library (one floor above the new installation), visitors are greeted by an all-glass entrance into an open lobby with a 13.5-foot ceiling. Self-service, express checkout units just inside the front doors make it quick and easy to borrow and renew library materials with an ID card. Four key services are housed on the entrance level. The General Information Desk, where visitors ask questions about the building, campus, and community, is conveniently located as one enters and near the five elevators that carry visitors to a variety of services and collections in the "Tower." Access Services (Circulation Services and Stacks Management) is located straight ahead past the elevators. This department assists users with loans, returns, renewals, holds, recalls, bills, fines, and pickup of materials requested through inter-library loan and other delivery services. Circulation Services also manages the lost-and-found and the study carrels. Stacks Management locates missing items and maintains the stacks.

The Procrastination Station café opened in February 2005 and serves approximately 10,000 visitors each month with beverages, pastries, sand-wiches, and salads. Its hours closely approximate those of the building. The café was named by an under-graduate student majoring in animal science through a contest conducted in April 2005. Across from the Procrastination Station are four quick-lookup PCs.

The Building Operations Desk is not really a ser-vice desk, but it is the home base for a team of staff and student assistants operating under the supervi-sion of the library's assistant director for adminis-trative services (Facilities and Business Office) who patrol the building during all open hours to ensure safety, monitor and report maintenance issues, and assist with all building-related issues. Staff at this desk respond to security gate alarms and assist with the 3M express checkout units when Circulation Services is closed.

Visitors use any of five elevators or three sets of stairs to travel down one level to the largest por-tion of the library and the primary space for the Learning Commons. Users can access the wireless network on the entrance and lower levels as well as the second and third floors of the Tower. All of this student-centered space is open on a first-come, first-served basis without time limits.

Once on the lower level, visitors are greeted with an individual lounge seating area and six tables for four, with power for laptop use on the wireless net-work. Furnishings and power poles in this area can be removed for events. Important events such as the grand opening, Friends of the Library dinner, and honorary degree awards have been held here. The comfortable seating area is flanked on three sides by structural brick columns lined with exhibit cases. The Library Arts and Exhibits Committee schedules monthly dis-plays throughout the year. South of the columns are fifty-eight individual workstations for public access to web browsers, productivity software, and library resources. Beyond these stations are floor-to-ceiling windows that look out onto the Courtyard.

To the left of the fifty-eight workstations is the Learning Commons and Technical Support Desk (LC Desk), the center for questions and answers in the Learning Commons and for technology support for the campus. Whenever the building is open, the LC Desk is staffed with experts from the library and two departments of the Office of Information Technologies (OIT), Computer Classrooms and Help Desk. Highly trained and customer-focused staff and student assistants are available to assist with questions about policies, hardware, software, peripherals, student accounts, online learning and course management systems, and anything else a user cares to ask. These experts teach users how to print, copy, scan, add to the debit account on their ID card, purchase from the office supply vending machine, or use any of the resources and services available through the Learning Commons. Workers check out diskette and CD drives for the public workstations, clean the workstations, and rove every 15 minutes to see if anyone needs help. The desk is staffed with three to six persons, a mix of staff and student assistants depending on demand and time of day.

Extending along the entire east wall of the open space are nine glass study rooms, each of which comfortably seats six. Groups of three or more have priority to use these rooms, which feature dry-erase boards and one computer (plus additional power and network access). Between the study rooms and the Courtyard are clusters of study pods. Each of the fifty tabletops offers one workstation but seats two to three. In addition, the area features six wired tables for groups of six or more to collaborate and eight individual workstations. Sixteen of the 103 authenticated workstations in this area are Macs. Students may use four scanners. Many students bring their own laptops to plug in or use on the wireless network.

Partway down the east side is the joint Academic Advising Link/Career Services Desk. This desk has two seats and workstations that enable the student assistants or advising/career services staff to access the systems they use in their primary office in another building. Students may use the desk and computers when the service providers are not working. Staffed hours are late afternoon and evening to coincide with the highest use of the Learning Commons by students. The Academic Advising Link provides comprehensive advising for undeclared students until they have selected a major, school, or college, including information about general education requirements, course registration, special learning opportunities, degree progress audits, student record accounts, domestic exchange programs, international programs, and other academic support services. Career Services provides information on field experience opportunities, job applications, job search, resume preparation, and interviewing with potential employers.

Along the southeast edge of the Learning Commons is the Calipari Room, named after former men's basketball coach John Calipari and his wife Ellen, who together donated $100,000. Librarians teach instruction and information literacy sessions here, and other Learning Commons service providers hold programs and workshops. Career Services offers resume-writing and job-search workshops each semester. The Writing Center offers a variety of specialized writing workshops such as how to write a personal statement and how to take a blue book exam. When the Learning Commons is crowded and the room is not scheduled for other purposes, it is open and staffed for drop-in use by students. The room provides nineteen student PC workstations and two teacher/monitor workstations.

In the southeast corner of the floor are four glass study rooms used in the late afternoon and evening by the Writing Center for 30-minute appointments with undergraduate and graduate writing tutors. These drop-in sessions are open to all members of the UMass Amherst community for assistance with all types of writing projects. A small print collection of writing resource books is available for in-building use in the area. The Writing Center is unique in the facility because students are free to use the space, except during the 23 hours per week when the Writing Center is staffed. The popularity of the service in its first year of operation (the total number of sessions the Writing Center provided tripled) led to the addition of summer hours and expanded hours in the second academic year.

Moving west along the south end are study tables and twenty individual PC workstations for those with UMass Amherst NetID (campus e-mail) accounts to access licensed software. The southwest corner of the lower level features a large open space configured for any type of event for groups of fifty or more. Since its opening, the Learning Commons has been in great demand as a place to hold lectures, panels, multimedia presentations, teleconferences, resource fairs, dinners, and tours. Campus groups may schedule events as long as they do not interfere with peak study periods.

Turning the southwest corner of the floor around the Courtyard to walk north, one passes the microform collections and study tables. Farther west is the Periodicals and Microforms Room, which is staffed most of the hours the building is open and holds the current issues of academic journals, popular magazines, and newspapers. Equipment for viewing and printing from microforms is near the desk. Farther north is the Interlibrary Loan and Document Delivery Office.

East of the Interlibrary Loan Office is the reference collection of 18,000 volumes. Farther east is the Reference and Research Assistance Desk, staffed exclusively by professional librarians. Here users receive individualized and in-depth assistance to complete their research successfully. East of the Reference and Research Assistance Desk, one returns to the fifty-eight public workstations and their printers. Students queue for open workstations in this area and collect printouts.

Information Commons Service Transaction Statistics

Each service point collects its own use statistics. Because the facility with its reconfigured or new services has not been open long, metrics have not yet stabilized. The library portion of the Learning Commons and Technical Support Desk answered 60,000 questions from September 7, 2005, to June 30, 2006. The OIT Help Desk answered 2,000 questions. During the same period, the Reference and Research Assistance Desk answered 18,000 questions that came in through face-to-face or phone contact with the desk, and the General Information Desk answered 17,500 questions.

Information Commons Staffing and Training

The Learning Commons and Technical Support Desk is the hub of service on the lower level and responds to general and technology inquiries. This service point is staffed all hours the building is open (along with the Building Operations Desk on the entrance level). It features a unique blend of staffing by three different groups: the library with 3.5 FTE dedicated classified staff, 3 staff from other areas who help out a few hours each week, and 7 FTE student assistants; OIT Computer Classrooms with 4.25 FTE student assistants; and OIT Help Desk with 1 FTE staff and 3 FTE student assistants. Learning Commons Desk workers rove every 15 minutes in maroon T-shirts and nametags that identify their service affiliation to assist users and to check for problems or unattended items. Staff and student assistants who staff the library side of the Learning Commons and Technical Support Desk are hired for their customer service and communication skills, flexibility, quick thinking, and interest in and aptitude for mastering new technologies on the fly.

The Reference and Research Assistance Desk is staffed by 12 FTE professional reference librarians with subject expertise and one highly experienced, paraprofessional coordinator. All student assistants who formerly worked at the reference desk were shifted to the Learning Commons and Technical Support Desk when the Learning Commons opened. The Periodicals and Microforms Room, as well as Interlibrary Loan and Document Delivery, were preexisting services and maintained their former staffing levels and functions. Other services such as Academic Advising, Career Services, and the Writing Center dispatch staff from their primary locations in other buildings to staff their open hours in the Learning Commons. Each of these units increased student assistant staffing through requests to their campus administrators for additional funding to support the new service point.

Each service point trains its own staff and student assistants. To facilitate active referral throughout the Learning Commons, cross-training orientation sessions are provided by each service provider for the other services during the summer. The coordinator of the Learning Commons schedules meetings of all service providers to discuss issues and provide training. A listserv is used to distribute updated information on changes in services and policies, as well as events, to all service providers. Library Learning Commons and Technical Support Desk staff and student assistants are kept updated as they work a 24/5 schedule through a blog maintained by the day supervisor and through intranet and e-mail postings. Intensive training and coordination is required to operate the Learning Commons and Technical Support Desk efficiently and effectively. Administrative and front-line managers for the library, OIT Computer Classrooms, and OIT Help Desk meet weekly to discuss issues, technologies, policies, staffing, and training. Training is ongoing; however, intensive student assistant training takes place in August each year for all groups working at this desk. Training sessions include desk procedures; workstation cleaning procedures and schedule; roving; policies; customer service;

reference interview; Learning Commons website; library website, intranet, and blog; OIT website and documentation; library catalog searching; databases; library and OIT workstation troubleshooting; printer, copier, UCard vending machine, and scanner use, troubleshooting, and maintenance; and typical software questions. During the summer of 2005, the Libraries' User Services Division adopted standardized "Customer Service Guidelines and Employment Parameters" that are emphasized with all new staff and student assistants and reviewed each year with all public services staff. Customer service training is provided in the library at least once per year.

The Learning Commons and Technical Support Desk has six workers during the busy daytime and evening hours and three workers during the midnight–8:00 a.m. Sunday–Thursday shift. Since staff come from three different departments and have specialized expertise, they practice what is referred to as the "invisible handoff." A student or other user approaches the desk and asks a question of the first worker with whom he or she makes eye contact, a student assistant or staff member from any of the three areas. The worker attempts to answer the question, but other workers who are not otherwise engaged listen as well and join the conversation to ensure a quick and accurate response to the question. Staff learn from one another and are able to answer that question themselves the next time it is asked. Students quickly learned that the Learning Commons and Technical Support Desk is the place to get technology and general help, both inside the Learning Commons and on the campus as a whole.

What's on the Desktop

All workstations in the Learning Commons feature web browsers, the Microsoft Office suite of productivity software, and several free programs. The fifty-eight PCs for public and Four College (Amherst, Hampshire, Mount Holyoke, and Smith Colleges) users do not require authentication and print to either monochrome or color printers with a guest payment card. The seventeen Gateway M280 tablet PCs available on four-hour loan to students from the third-floor Reserves/Media Desk also have this software image, although students must authenticate onto the wireless network using their NetID. A scanner is available with Twain software. The 103 workstations (sixteen Macs and eighty-seven PCs) on the lower level, as well as the nineteen PCs in the Calipari Room, offer the entire package of software licensed by UMass Amherst by OIT Computer Classrooms. These workstations are limited to use by current students, faculty, and staff with a campus NetID. Students, faculty, and staff pay for printing and copying with a debit account on their campus ID card, the UCard. Five scanners and three printers serve the 122 workstations in this area. Categories of software provided on the authenticated workstations include operating system, antivirus, assistive technologies, browser, desktop, developer tools, educational packages, library helper applications, multimedia, plug-ins, SFTP and SSH, statistical, utilities, and web authoring. Consult http://www.oit.umass.edu/classrooms/software/index.html for a complete list of the current software packages licensed for students, faculty, and staff. Licenses are reviewed and renewed each year based on input from campus constituents.

Information Commons Assessment

Many of the services and features incorporated into the UMass Amherst Learning Commons surfaced from the open-ended comments submitted when UMass Libraries conducted LibQUAL+ in spring 2004. A one-page summary derived from a content analysis of the comments guided the planning team. A focus group of student employees from the service providers for the Learning Commons met while the renovations were under way and generated the names for the service points on the entrance and lower levels of the building. A one-day paper-and-pencil questionnaire distributed on the lower level captured initial demographics of users of the Learning Commons and their comments on November 14, 2005. Another paper-and-pencil questionnaire given at the entrance to the building on March 14, 2006, determined where users went in the twenty-six-story building as well as demographics, satisfaction with existing facilities and services, and interest in potential services. Focus groups and individual interviews were conducted with users of the Learning Commons in April 2006 to determine which furnishing types they preferred and to solicit feedback on the extent to which the facility was meeting student needs. A survey of the types of questions presented at the Reference and Research Assistance Desk and how long users spent at the desk was followed by a focus group to gather user perspectives on the new model of reference assistance provided in the Learning Commons. Seating sweeps (two weeks every hour on the half hour for fall 2005; four weeks every hour on the half hour during spring 2006) measured occupancy of each section of the space throughout the 24-hour day as well as personal laptop presence (on average 12 percent of users have brought their own laptops since the Learning Commons opened) in comparison to a baseline survey of the same space conducted in 2001. Future assessment plans include pop-up surveys on workstations in the Learning Commons and telephone/e-mail interviews conducted by a campus assessment group. Standard metrics of the types of questions asked in person and by phone are gathered at each service point in the building.

Users are encouraged by staff of the Learning Commons to submit suggestions on the comment form prominently located on the Learning Commons website. A wooden suggestion box just inside the main entrance to the building is a popular way for users to submit written feedback.

Information Commons Governance

The Provost's Learning Commons Committee was established by the provost in spring 2005 and is presently chaired by the faculty advisor to the provost for undergraduate education. Members include many of the same individuals from the Learning Commons Core Planning Group (described below) who represent the library, OIT, and Information Technology Minor Program, along with the chief information officer and the deputy provost. The Provost's Committee guided the construction and launch of the UMass Amherst Learning Commons and now provides administrative, budgetary, policy, and visioning for both ongoing operations and future expansion plans.

The coordinator of the Learning Commons and Undergraduate Library Services, a librarian, communicates with and coordinates the efforts of the academic support services that operate in the Learning Commons: Learning Commons and Technical Support Desk, OIT Help Desk and Computer Classrooms, Writing Center, Academic Advising Link, Career Services, Learning Resource Center, Reserves, Reference and Research Assistance, Periodicals/Microforms, and General Information. Communication with these groups is through a listserv and periodic meetings and training sessions. The Learning Commons and Technical Support Desk groups (Library and OIT Help Desk and Computer Classrooms) meet weekly to manage the primary source of technology and library support. The coordinator is the direct supervisor for the staff who operate the library side of the Learning Commons and Technical Support Desk. In addition, this key librarian coordinates information literacy services to undergraduates.

Lessons Learned

▌ The IC model of service meets the needs and wants of today's undergraduates. To accomplish these goals requires cooperation across the campus. Such cooperation involves turf battles along with concerns about whose budget benefits from the joint effort and who receives the credit for the success. We must focus continually on the fact that no one group can build and maintain an information commons alone and that it requires all of us working together to meet the needs of our new students. Since our commons is located in the library, we always share the credit with all those campus units who have worked hard to make it a wonderful campus resource.

▌ We found it successful to provide a variety of spaces to meet a variety of needs. We need to be attentive to how usage changes through continuous assessment and adaptation of services and facilities.

▌ The information commons has transformed and enhanced the image of the library on campus and in the region. We thought the facility would be a hit with students, but we had no idea of its positive impact of the perception of the library, OIT, Writing Center, and the other service providers.

▌ Clearly articulated policies are extremely important.

UNIVERSITY OF MINNESOTA–TWIN CITIES

WILSON LIBRARY

Prepared June 2006 by Caroline Crouse (Information Literacy Librarian)

Library website	http://www.lib.umn.edu
IC website	http://www.lib.umn.edu/about/undergrad/infocommons/
Carnegie classification	Research Universities (very high research activity)
# Undergraduates	28,957
# Graduate students	14,107
# Faculty	2,495
Highest degree offered	Doctorate
# Volumes	6,200,669
# Periodical titles	36,900
# FTE librarians	0.25
# Other FTE staff	0.75
Annual circulation	591,397
Annual gate entries	373,628
IC opening date	November 11, 2004
IC name	Information Commons
IC service model type	Single-staffed by librarians, paraprofessional, or students—somewhat integrated services
# Computer workstations	35
What's on desktop	Internet, proprietary research databases, office suites, word processing, spreadsheet, charting/graphing, desktop publishing, graphics, mathematics/statistics, multimedia/presentation
IC architect	Sylvia Frank–Carlsen Frank Architects
Hours	Staffed: Mon.–Thurs. 9:00 a.m.–10:00 p.m.; Fri. 9:00 a.m.–6:00 p.m.; Sat. 12:00 p.m.–6:00 p.m.; Sun. 12:00 p.m.–10:00 p.m. Building: Mon.–Thurs. 8:00 a.m.–12:00 a.m.; Fri. 8:00 a.m.–9:00 p.m.; Sat. 10:00 a.m.–10:00 p.m.; Sun. 12:00 p.m.–12:00 a.m.
IC area	1,735 sq. ft.
# Physical service points in IC	1
Print reference materials in the IC?	Yes, computer help books. IC shares the first floor of Wilson Library with the reference collection, so there are many print resources nearby (just not physically within the IC). Students can bring materials into the IC without checking them out.

Location of Institution and Campus Description

Founded in 1851 as the state's land grant institution, the University of Minnesota is one of the state's greatest assets and one of the most comprehensive universities in the United States. The University of Minnesota system has four campuses, of which the Twin Cities campus is the largest. Nestled in the heart of the urban environment of Minneapolis and St. Paul, the campus covers more than 1,200 acres and has more than 50,000 students.

The Twin Cities campus has a full range of academic programs from liberal arts to agriculture. The campus also includes a medical school, law school, and business school, all highly ranked.

Information Commons Description

The Information Commons is on the first floor of Wilson Library directly in front of the main library entrance. It is enclosed by a front glass wall, a side glass and opaque wall, and on the other two sides by the library's structural walls. The computers are arranged in row fashion, with enough space at each table for at least two individuals working on a project. There is one information desk within the Commons, in the back corner of the room.

The Information Commons houses thirty-six workstations, including

- thirty-two productivity PCs and two productivity iMacs with CD burners
- one multimedia PC and one multimedia Mac with Epson scanner and DVD/CD burner
- two digital camcorders
- three external hard drives
- one Flash memory card reader
- one monochrome/color printer

Additionally, the Commons has an ADA-compliant station with an adjustable-height desk and special software for patrons with disabilities. There is also a Center for Writing satellite area within the Commons equipped with a computer and a separate consulting table.

The first floor of Wilson Library also holds the library's general reference desk, which is outside the Commons. The desk and reference room have eight additional computers without productivity software for library research.

Information Commons Service Transaction Statistics

In 2005/2006, 6,256 questions were asked, including directional, research, and technology reference questions.

Information Commons Staffing and Training

The Information Commons has a single-staffing model, staffed by a combination of four librarians, one paraprofessional, and five student workers all cross-trained in library research and some multimedia support. The Commons is staffed and open 77 hours per week. During several hours per week, the Commons attendant (either paraprofessional or librarian) also monitors chat reference, an arrangement that helps allow chat service to operate an additional 12 hours per week.

When recruiting student workers, we try to find those who are either proficient in multimedia software or have experience working in the university libraries. We pay significantly higher than many of the other student jobs within the library, which helps attract highly skilled students. For technology training, students work on self-paced training modules for scanning, Microsoft Office, and video editing. For research training, the students attend Information Literacy and RefWorks workshops and complete an online library tutorial. Librarians receive training in Microsoft Office and scanning; however, the time demands on the trainer and the trainee led us to work on a referral system for advanced technology instruction.

The paraprofessional and one librarian have advanced multimedia skills and serve as a backup for desk workers who may not have knowledge of these applications.

We are currently developing an online training module on searching in the library catalog and common databases.

What's on the Desktop

Standard PCs (28): Internet Explorer, MS Office (f), Photoshop Elements, GoLive, Firefox, WinSCP3, Magnifier

SPSS PCs (3): Internet Explorer, MS Office (f), Photoshop Elements, GoLive, Firefox, WinSCP3, Magnifier, SPSS

Multimedia PC (1): Internet Explorer, WinSCP3, Epson Scan, ABBYY FineReader, MS Office (f), Acrobat Pro, Firefox, Scanner Reference

iMacs (2): GoLive, Photoshop Elements, FTP (f), MS Office (f)

Multimedia Mac (1): Graphic Design (f), MS Office (f), Web Design (f), FTP (f), Video Production (f), FineReader Sprint

Information Commons Assessment

At the University of Minnesota Information Commons, we developed a thorough assessment plan that commenced prior to the development of the Commons and will continue through the first year and beyond. Our assessment tools include a short pop-up survey, a twelve-question paper survey, focus groups with undergraduate students, gate counts for Wilson Library, a software request notebook, statistics for reference and technology questions, and all questions asked at the information desk for two-week periods in the middle and end of the semester. By varying the assessment tools, we capture both in-depth responses through the long survey and focus groups and a large response rate from the less time- and resource-intensive assessment tools such as the pop-up survey and gate counts. Results from the survey are included in our first-year report: http://staff.lib.umn.edu/ug/IC/reports/firstyear-report/.

Information Commons Governance

The Information Commons is managed by one librarian (approximately 25 percent of time spent at the Commons) and one 0.75 FTE paraprofessional.

Lessons Learned

▌ Everything should move! Chairs are always getting rearranged, and desks would as well if they could. The perfect information commons would include many laptops as well as desks and chairs on wheels and no walls.

▌ Build space for about twice as many students as you think will use the facility. Our Information Commons has truly been an "if you build it, they will come" type of experience. We hit capacity on the first day and have waiting lines pretty frequently, even though there are several large computer labs nearby. Establishing "room to grow" is important.

▌ Listen to your students. We distributed a couple of surveys and held focus groups for the Information Commons four months after it opened and learned a lot about what we were doing well, what we should be doing, and what we should stop.

UNIVERSITY OF NORTH CAROLINA AT CHARLOTTE

J. MURREY ATKINS LIBRARY,
UNIVERSITY OF NORTH CAROLINA AT CHARLOTTE

Prepared June 2006 by D. Russell Bailey, Ph.D. (UNCC Associate University Librarian for the Information Commons) and Barbara Gunter Tierney (Information Commons Desk Coordinator)

Library website	http://library.uncc.edu
IC website	http://library.uncc.edu/infocommons/
Carnegie classification	Doctoral/Research Universities
# Undergraduates	19,100
# Graduate students	4,000
# Faculty	3,100 general faculty (1,500 academic faculty, 1,600 administrative professionals)
Highest degree offered	Doctorate
# Volumes	1,000,000
# Periodical titles	14,000
# FTE librarians	30 for entire library, 11.5 for IC
# Other FTE staff	70 for entire library, 5.5 for IC
Library annual budget	$7,200,000 (no separate budget for the continuing operation of the IC)
Annual circulation	159,000
Annual gate entries	890,000
IC opening date	1999
IC name	J. Murrey Atkins Library Information Commons
IC service model type	Partially integrated services
# Computer workstations	291 PCs and Macintoshes
What's on desktop	Internet, proprietary research databases, office suites, word processing, spreadsheet, charting/graphing, desktop publishing, graphics, mathematics/statistics, multimedia/presentation
IC architect	Shepley Bulfinch Richardson & Abbott
Hours	All hours the library is open: Mon.–Thurs. 7:30 a.m.–12:00 a.m.; Fri. 7:30 a.m.–8:00 p.m.; Sat. 10:00 a.m.–8:00 p.m.; Sun. 11:00 a.m.–12:00 a.m.
IC area	97,752 sq. ft. (area devoted to public computer space: 11,600 sq. ft. main floor; 2,900 sq. ft. second floor; 600 sq. ft. third floor)
# Physical service points in IC	4
Average # IC users in a typical month	12,216 (146,589 user contacts per twelve-month year)
Print reference materials in the IC?	Yes, the main print reference collection for the library.

Location of Institution and Campus Description

The University of North Carolina at Charlotte is the fourth-largest of sixteen campuses within the UNC system. With a student-faculty ratio of 16 to 1, it serves 19,000 undergraduate and 4,000 graduate students who hail from forty-eight states and seventy-eight other countries.

Founded in 1946 as Charlotte College, UNC Charlotte was designated a doctoral research institution in 2000. The campus features modern architecture surrounded by landscaped walks and trails. Campus focal points include outstanding botanical gardens (VanLandingham Glen), the McMillan Greenhouse, and the ten-story J. Murrey Atkins Library. The UNC Charlotte campus is located on Highway 49, eight miles northeast of downtown Charlotte.

Information Commons Description

The J. Murrey Atkins Library Information Commons opened in spring 1999 and provides an integrated continuum of library services and technology for students, faculty, staff, and community patrons. The Information Commons is a blend of refurbished space and new construction on the first floor of the library, with additional areas of networked computers on the second and third floors. A virtual tour of the Commons and library is available at http://dlib.uncc.edu/tours/virtual/.

Library patrons entering the Information Commons are greeted by a welcoming open space featuring a three-story atrium. The first-floor Commons occupies approximately 97,000 square feet. In all, the Commons provides more than 290 public computers, many of which are arranged in circular pods (housing eight computers apiece) throughout the facility. A detailed location breakdown of these public computers shows 107 PCs in the first-floor open space; eight PCs in the first-floor Scanning Lab; six Macs in the first-floor Multimedia Lab; sixty-eight PCs in the second-floor open space; eight PCs in the third-floor open space; seven PCs in stack areas; three PCs in group study rooms; two PCs in the Disability Assistive Technology Room; fifty circulating laptops; twenty laptops in the Mobile Classroom; and twenty laptops in the Electronic Classroom.

The formal Commons consists of five sections whose heads/coordinators report directly to the head of the Commons: Information Desk, Presentation Support Services, Reference Services, Research Data Services, and Instructional Services. Four desks—Information, Presentation Support, Reference, and Circulation—provide public service on the first floor, and the Collections public service desk is on the second floor.

At the functional center of the Information Commons is the Information Desk. This desk serves as the first point of service library patrons encounter upon entering the building. It provides basic information on all services and resources within the library as well as general information about the university. Information Desk staff are trained to provide informed referrals to other desks, locations, or specialized staff if a patron's query moves from basic to a higher level of complexity. The Information Desk is also the repository of library information (UNCC publications, directories, schedules, specialty resources) and assists with library security functions, monitors printing and photocopying machine problems, books group study rooms, and provides the headquarters for nighttime manager-on-duty activities. This desk is staffed by a team of two full-time paraprofessionals, nine part-time students, and four staff volunteers.

The Presentation Support Desk provides resources and technology assistance for patrons' production/presentation activities in various media (print, sound, and still and moving images). Presentation Support staff provide assistance with software at point-of-need, because there currently is no general place for students to go on campus to learn software. (Campus IT offers software classes for faculty and staff, but not for students. Some specialized software, such as SPSS and GIS, are taught by the faculties.) Technology resources are accessible in public areas and in specialty and staff-mediated labs—Multimedia, Video/Audio, Scanning, and the Adaptive Technology Lab for disabled patrons. Presentation Support staff assist library patrons with scanning, word processing, audiovisual production, and related activities. This desk is staffed by one full-time and one half-time paraprofessional and a team of students.

Reference Services provides traditional and technology-enhanced services. The Reference Unit serves as a guide to a wide range of online resources as well as the print reference collection (shelved in the first-floor Commons) and the print general collections (shelved on seven floors of the library). Librarians and staff who make up the Reference Unit serve scheduled hours at the Reference Desk, which is the front line in teaching students and other patrons how to best utilize online bibliographic databases and electronic full-text resources, journals, newspapers, books, and government documents. Members of the Reference Unit also teach large numbers of classes, create innovative websites and class web pages, and generate user guides for students. They are also integral participants in the Library's Liaison Outreach Program to academic departments and particular populations of students (e.g., transfer students, adult/evening students, and disability students). Virtual reference chat is offered through the Southeast Research Libraries consortium. Reference Services is staffed by twelve full-time librarians, two full-time paraprofessionals, and two students.

Research Data Services provides resources and direct support to the campus community for machine-readable data needs. Research Data Services staff assist researchers by identifying available data, obtaining data through memberships or purchase, reformatting data into usable formats for researchers, and assisting researchers in manipulating and presenting data in a variety of formats. Research Data Services staff also produce end products (such as datasets and maps) for instructional support. This service is staffed by two full-time librarians and one full-time paraprofessional.

Instructional Services provides educational support in library services and resources to the campus community. It uses two instruction class-rooms within Atkins Library, one room with twenty laptops available for hands-on-instruction and the other with an instructor demonstration terminal. A twenty-unit mobile wireless laptop classroom provides an additional option. Instructional Services is staffed by a full-time instruction librarian who assists in coordinating the instructional work of twelve reference librarians (and other librarians). These librarians provide instruction that is primarily assignment specific and oriented toward research processes for all levels of the university curriculum. Although there is no formal information literacy program, there are multiple library instruction classes taught for English 101 and Freshman Seminar. The librarians also focus on instruction for particular populations such as transfer students, adult/evening students, and disability students. Subject specialist librarians do a great deal of subject-specific instruction.

Information Commons
Special Facilities

Immediately adjacent to the Information Commons is UNCC's Video Production Services Unit, which provides videoconferencing and distance learning connectivity to the university through the North Carolina Research and Education Network, the North Carolina Information Highway, and the use of H.323 or ISDN communication protocols.

Displayed on the walls of the Information Commons is the UNCC art collection, which features original oil and watercolor paintings, drawings, photographs, and other works. Glass display cases strategically positioned throughout the Commons provide constantly changing displays featuring the library's varied collections.

The Ritazza Cafe (equipped with public computer workstations) is located on the ground-floor level of the library.

Information Commons Service
Transaction Statistics

The number of service transactions or users at the various public service desks in the Commons is recorded. There are 146,589 patron contacts per year, or an average of 12,216 contacts per month.

Information Commons Staffing and Training

The Information Commons is staffed all hours the library is open to the public. Staff positions were created through a mix of new library and computer center positions, redefined job descriptions of existing staff, and reassigned staff from other departments.

Staffing is a mix of 11.5 FTE reference/research data services librarians, 1.5 IT staff, 4 FTE support staff, and 4.5 FTE student assistants. Normally two people are assigned at each desk each hour of the day, except for single-staff coverage during early morning and late night periods. The Commons is staffed 87 hours per week by full-time librarians, 20 hours by part-time librarians, 101 hours by library support staff, and 101 hours by student assistants. At times staff rove the Commons assisting patrons. Commons staff self-identify to library patrons and do not wear special badges or uniforms.

Training, both primary and ongoing, is essential to the functional success of the Information Commons public service desks. Training is also of primary importance in creating a collaborative attitude among Commons staff. To begin the process of staff training, the Atkins Library Public Services Committee coordinated the creation of general public service desk basic competencies. Later, this same committee coordinated the creation of second-level, desk-specific competencies.

In addition, a series of in-house cross-training classes was organized and coordinated by the Information Commons Planning Group and Instructional Services and offered to all interested library staff. These classes included training on how to do a reference interview; introduction to key library databases; introduction to the library catalog; basic computer troubleshooting; basic peripheral troubleshooting (e.g., printers, scanners, network cards); customer service; library policies and procedures; basic library information (e.g., hours,

directions, services, referrals); Internet searching; and basics of specific software applications. In addition, trainers from each public service desk and library unit gave instruction on the types of services offered by that unit or desk. Tutorials covering class content are posted on the intranet pages of the library's website, and the scheduling of additional classes is ongoing to ensure that everyone's competency skills remain current, with content revised as technology changes.

What's on the Desktop

Approximately 90 percent of Commons computers allow access to productivity software (e.g., spreadsheet, word processing/text editing, charting/graphing, desktop publishing, graphics, mathematics/statistics, multimedia/presentation, scanning, utilities) as well as to the Internet and the library's proprietary research databases. This productivity software is provided through campus site licenses, so the library's public computers have the same software as campus labs.

There is no productivity software on the thirty workstations directly adjacent to the Reference Desk so that they will be more readily available to staff assisting users with research questions. These reference workstations all provide access to the Internet and the library's proprietary research databases. Printing is available on all networked public computers in the library and requires payment with a copy card.

Information Commons Assessment

The library's management team conducts formal and informal assessment to determine if current resources are meeting the informational and instructional needs of library users. The assessment results allow the management team to adjust services and direct resources to maintain and update the infrastructure. In addition, desk statistics are taken at all public service desks and are reviewed and discussed on a regular basis, as is informal feedback from library users.

The LibQUAL+ and Project SAILS instruments have provided recent formal assessment for Atkins Library as a whole. The LibQUAL+ assessment was conducted in 2003. LibQUAL+ defined and measured library service quality by surveying library users' perceptions of service quality—identifying gaps between desired, perceived, and minimum expectations of service. The Project SAILS assessment was conducted in 2004. SAILS assessed the information literacy skills of UNCC students.

Information Commons Governance

The Information Commons is the heart of the library and is under the direction of the associate university librarian for the Information Commons, who reports directly to the university librarian. The university librarian meets regularly with the UNCC provost for academic affairs and the Deans' Council to ensure that the activities of the Commons and library mesh with the academic goals of the university as a whole.

In addition, the Faculty Advisory Library Committee consists of representatives from UNCC's academic departments and serves as an advising body to the university librarian. Also, the Atkins Library Public Services Committee consists of representatives of all library departments and units and serves as an advising body to the university librarian and the library's managers' group.

The Faculty Center for Teaching and e-Learning, which occupies a first-floor suite of offices adjacent to the Information Commons, within the library building, is governed by UNCC's Information and Technology Services department.

At UNCC, five-year academic strategic plans are updated and regenerated every two years. This same strategic planning activity is also implemented in the Atkins Library Information Commons with the creation of a vision/mission/goals/objectives document that is regularly updated. In addition, several in-house committees exist to implement initiatives and expedite planning and problem solving in the Commons.

The Information Commons Planning Group existed from 1998 to 2002 and was an essential component of Commons initiatives and implementation. The group originally consisted of the three formal Commons section heads. Over time, it evolved in makeup, size, and function as a Commons integrating mechanism that represented the "enhanced Commons," including not only the formal Commons but also representatives from every section of the library (Systems, Access and Outreach Services, Collections and Technical Services, and Special Collections). The Information Commons Planning Group met monthly and was responsible for developing all Commons resource and service plans and policies. It received and transmitted communications and input in all formats (Commons website, Commons listserv, face-to-face meetings, hard copy communiqués) and distributed regular meeting minutes library-wide.

In December 2002, after the Information Desk had been in existence for eighteen months, the Information Commons Planning Group was absorbed by the Atkins Library Public Services Committee, which currently meets once a month and deals with all issues involving public service, including Information Commons issues. This committee is chaired by the associate university librarian for the Information Commons, who reports to the university librarian. Membership includes professionals, paraprofessionals, and students from all library public service units.

In addition, the Information Desk Coordinating Team and the Presentation Support Desk Coordinating Team handle initiatives, issues, and problems involving their respective desks. Although these teams meet separately, they have much overlap in membership.

Lessons Learned

▌ We currently have too many public service desks. We have the Information Desk, Reference Desk, Presentation Support Desk, and Circulation Desk all within steps of each other on the first floor. It is difficult to staff so many desks all the hours the library is open to the public, and it is confusing for patrons to know which desk to visit for help with their various questions. We may need to replace four separate desks with a "one-stop-shopping superdesk" or find other ways of combining service points.

▌ We invested too much in expensive, nonmoveable, mill-worked furnishings that contribute to a nonflexible working environment. We should have opted for modular units that could be configured in various ways to respond to evolving patron needs.

▌ The three-story atrium provides beautiful natural light but also funnels noise from the first floor to the second and third floors.

▌ Pillars obstruct sightlines between service points.

UNIVERSITY OF SOUTHERN CALIFORNIA

THOMAS AND DOROTHY LEAVEY LIBRARY

Prepared June 2006 by Shahla Bahavar, Ph.D. (Reference Coordinator, USC Libraries)

Library website	http://www.usc.edu/leavey/
IC website	http://www.usc.edu/leavey/ic/
Carnegie classification	Research Universities (very high research activity)
# Undergraduates	17,000
# Graduate Students	16,000
# Faculty	3,100 full-time, 1,400 part-time
Highest degree offered	Doctorate
# Volumes	Leavey 39,000, USC Libraries 3.9 million, e-books 280,351, e-journals 37,712, databases 53,756
# Periodical titles	Leavey 271, USC Libraries 37,800
# FTE librarians	5
# Other FTE staff	9
Library annual budget	$1,390,000
Annual circulation	130,000
Annual gate entries	1.5 million
IC opening date	1994
IC name	Lower IC: Leavey Upper IC: Dorothy Leavey
IC service model type	Primarily integrated service—reference/computing combined
# Computer workstations	250 PCs and Macs for both Commons: 88 PCs and 43 Macs in Lower IC, 74 PCs and 1 Mac in Upper IC, 20 PCs in PC classroom (Learning Room A), 24 Macs in Mac classroom (Learning Room B)
What's on desktop	Library research resources, proprietary databases, Internet, Microsoft Office, spreadsheet, web publishing, Adobe suite, mathematics/statistical package (SPSS, SAS, Minitab, etc.), graphics, charting, multimedia/presentation, and class applications, e.g., SAP 2000, ARCVIEW, Screen Writer, AUTOCAD, Finale, EP Budgeting, EP Scheduling, Mathlab
IC architect	Shepley Bulfinch Richardson & Abbott
Hours	24/7 during fall and spring, cutbacks in summer
IC area	Lower IC 18,998 sq. ft., Upper IC 9,892 sq. ft.
# Physical service points in IC	Lower IC 2, Upper IC 1
Average # IC users in a typical month	Lower IC 23,100, Upper IC 22,320
Print reference materials in the IC?	Yes, basic undergraduate reference collection.

Location of Institution and Campus Description

The University of Southern California, founded in 1880, is one of the largest research institutions on the West Coast. The main campus is adjacent to downtown Los Angeles and is the largest private employer in the city. The renaissance-style buildings are constructed around a series of plazas, fountains, and parks. The University Park Campus is home to the USC College of Letters, Arts and Sciences and many professional schools. The Health Sciences Campus is northeast of downtown Los Angeles and is home to the USC Keck School of Medicine, the School of Pharmacy, three major teaching hospitals, and programs in Occupational Science and Occupational Therapy and Biokinesiology and Physical Therapy. USC has programs and other centers in Marina Del Rey, Catalina Island, Alhambra, Orange County and elsewhere around Southern California and in Sacramento and Washington, D.C. USC is one of the top institutions in the nation with respect to diversity, with the largest international student enrollment in the United States; students come from all fifty states and nearly 150 countries. The average SAT score of the freshman class enrolled in 2004/2005 was 1350, with an average GPA of 4.0. The student-faculty ratio is 10 to 1. USC offers bachelor's degrees in eighty-nine undergraduate majors, along with master's, doctoral, and professional degrees in 236 areas of study.

Information Commons Description

Leavey Library is one of nineteen branch libraries at USC. It is the undergraduate library focused on fostering undergraduate teaching and learning. Although Leavey is geared to serve undergraduates, assessments document a high level of graduate student use of Leavey's information commons on regular basis. The two Leavey commons are high-technology environments that provide a place conducive to exploring knowledge in a variety of electronic and print formats.

The information commons are the most innovative and original aspect of the library's building and services. This is the place where a particularly high level of collaborative, intellectual activity occurs. The original commons, on the ground level of Leavey Library (called Lower Commons), opened as an integral part of the Leavey Library in August 1994. The Lower Commons occupies the entire ground level and includes two networked hands-on teaching classrooms (one PC and one Mac), an auditorium, and a centralized print center for all 250 computer workstations in the building. The two entrance/exit doors from the east and west wings of the huge rectangular room provide access to the Lower Commons. The bright color scheme used in every level of the building provides an attractive, pleasant work/study environment for library users.

At the center of the Lower Commons is the Research/Computing Consultation Desk. This open space invites students to consult one-on-one with the Commons desk staff on their research and computing needs. There are 131 computers (PC and Mac) in the Lower Commons. The workstations are clustered in pie-shaped pods (housing six computers in each pod) designed with space for two seats per station, with low dividers separating the desks and providing privacy for group collaboration on computer workstations. The integrated desktops provide access to library research resources, Internet, e-mail, and software applications. Per the software licensing agreement, the computers in the Commons are restricted to the USC community and require user authentication.

The Upper Commons, on the second floor, was established in 1998, four years after the opening of the original commons. Because of high demand for more computing workstations and in response to student calls for more collaborative workrooms, in 1998 the second floor was retrofitted to create this second commons (officially named the Dorothy Leavey Memorial Upper Information Commons). It is similar in design to the Lower Commons and has seventy-four PC workstations in the east wing. The west wing features forty wired laptop carrels with convenient electrical and network connections.

There are 250 networked computer workstations for students' use in Leavey. Twenty-five research workstations on the first floor provide access to Internet and electronic resources and Homer catalog for walk-in users. A scanner and photocopy machine are available in the Lower Commons. The building is wireless, with wireless hubs inside and out. In addition, numerous Ethernet access ports are available throughout the building for laptop connection.

Both Upper and Lower Commons have many group study rooms (thirty-four total). All collaborative workrooms provide whiteboard and network connection for laptop, and the Lower Commons collaborative workrooms have computers as well. Students may check out portable projectors to use in the collaborative workrooms for group presentations. Group study rooms are exclusively for student use, and room reservations can be made up to a week in advance. The Lower Commons collaborative workrooms come in two sizes: most rooms seat six to eight people; the three largest have seating capacity for fifteen to eighteen. The Upper Commons group study rooms are smaller than those in the Lower Commons (up to four people) but have windows and outside views, which many students prefer.

Reference service is available in person and by phone, e-mail, and chat. The integrated service desks in the Lower and Upper Commons provide basic research and computing assistance around the clock. Librarians provide in-depth research assistance and one-on-one consultation to students and faculty on locating information via electronic and print resources during scheduled hours at the Lower Commons desk. Student navigation assistants provide basic research/reference assistance, informational/directional help, and computing consultation at all times Leavey is open. Patrons may consult the Commons desk staff with research, computing, or information inquiries and expect to receive assistance from librarians, student navigation assistants, and other full-time staff. The mix of services and availability of a wide array of research and computing resources mean that students can pursue all phases of a given assignment without leaving the building and possibly without even leaving the Commons.

Two hands-on networked classrooms (Learning Room A and Learning Room B) provide an exceptional environment for teaching and learning. One is equipped with twenty PCs, the other with twenty-four Macs. Librarians and instructors work directly with students in these spaces and conduct information literacy sessions. These classrooms are also used for overflow if there is no class in session. There is also a multimedia auditorium to support teaching initiatives; this fifty-two-seat facility is ideal for lectures, presentations, and other teaching/learning situations. The PC classroom and the auditorium are also equipped with Personal Response System (a.k.a. "clicker") technology.

Adjacent to the Lower Commons desk, a centralized printing area handles remote printing from all networked computers throughout the library, including color printing. The Print Center is open 24 hours a day or at all times the library is open. Printing is fee-based and is paid by debiting discretionary accounts linked to students' USC ID cards. The Value Transfer Station, in the basement of Leavey Library by the Print Center, allows students to convert cash to discretionary funds on their USCard.

Around the perimeter of the Lower Commons is a basic/core print reference collection that merges digital resources with traditional resources of an undergraduate library. The desk reference collection at the Commons includes ready reference and fact-finding sources, current social issues sets, print periodical indexes, and software guides.

Information Commons Service Transaction Statistics

Leavey Library is the most heavily trafficked library on campus. The Commons desk/Reference desk statistics form logs questions fielded by categories, according to the question type (reference, computing, and informational/directional) and how it was received. There are separate statistics forms for librarians, staff, and student navigation assistants. The total transactions per month during a typical regular semester are 4,000. This number reflects the user contacts at the two Commons service desks but not at the other two public service desks in the library—the Print Center and circulation desk. In general, about 40 percent of the questions are reference, 40 percent computing, and 20 percent directional.

Information Commons Staffing and Training

The Information Commons desks are staffed at all hours of operation. There are different staffing models for the Lower and Upper Commons. Lower Commons is the library's main reference desk, with a staffing model that includes a mix of librarians, student navigation assistants, and full-time staff. Librarians and full-time staff, assisted by student assistants, provide advanced research service during scheduled hours. Student navigation assistants provide basic information and computing assistance at all hours; normally two are scheduled for each shift except the graveyard shift (midnight–8:00 a.m.), which is single-staffed.

The Upper Commons is solely staffed by student navigation assistants during all library hours. There is a structured referral process between the Upper and Lower Commons service desks. Advanced reference inquiries or in-depth research consultation requests from the Upper Commons are referred to librarians or professional staff in the Lower Commons.

A tiered service concept is at the heart of the reference model in the Leavey Information Commons. The services at both Commons are integrated so that patrons can receive research/reference assistance and computing consultation from the same desk, creating "one-stop shopping service." The integrated tiered service model draws upon the student navigation assistants to answer basic reference, informational, directional, and computing questions while referring more challenging questions to professional staff and librarians. The referral process from a student navigation assistant to staff member or librarian takes place intuitively. Patrons can approach the Commons desks with

any research/reference, information, or computing-related question. Any available staff at the desk may take the question. For hardware/software questions, librarians may either choose to field the request if they feel comfortable or refer it to one of the student navigation assistants, who are technologically skilled members of the Commons staff. Librarians may expect a similar referral strategy from student navigation assistants on reference queries.

We have designed a structured training program for student navigation assistants who work at the Commons desks. Upon completion of the hiring process, assistants are required to go through a comprehensive training program (10–15 training hours) before they are added to the schedule. The training period occurs at the beginning of each semester, with follow-up training toward mid-semester and a refresher at the beginning of a new semester for returning student assistants.

The training program consists of several modules. Each module covers a specific area, including administrative issues, general orientation to Leavey and other campus libraries, software applications, troubleshooting, Print Center training, and reference. Because of the proximity of the Print Center to the Lower Commons desk, student assistants go through a Print Center cross-training, so that in case of emergency they are prepared to provide assistance at the Print Center. The reference module encompasses four sections: reference interview, Library of Congress system, and reference services (in-person, virtual chat, and e-mail); electronic resources (databases, e-journals, e-books, full-text resources, Scholar's Portal); online catalogs; and print reference sources. Librarians, the Information Commons manager, the USC Libraries Information Technology staff, and computing consultants share in conducting the training sessions related to their specialties.

Besides the initial training, mid-semester follow-up sessions and early-semester refreshers orient students to recent developments and changes in the library system or introduce new electronic resources. The training program is reviewed and modified each year to enhance the content. To achieve this goal and to assess individual training needs and preferences, a training survey is conducted toward the end of the semester. The student navigation assistant assessment feedback provides input for the development of new modules or modifications to the training format.

What's on the Desktop

All the workstations in the two commons and wired classrooms provide access to the same rich collection of productivity software, including Microsoft Office, web publishing tools, graphics, statistical packages (SPSS, SAS, Mathlab, Minitab, etc.), class applications, Internet, and e-mail as well as library research tools, electronic databases, specialized resources, e-books, e-journals, full-text resources, and library catalogs. All of these workstations require USC account log-in for access.

The three public workstations in the Lower and Upper Commons as well as the twenty-five other public research workstations on the Leavey main floor provide access to Internet, e-mail, and library resources. There are no productivity software applications on these workstations. These workstations do not require USC user log-in and are designated for USC UNIX account activation, e-mail, electronic and print reserve materials access, electronic resources, and Homer (USC Library online catalog) usage.

Information Commons Assessment

Leavey strives to be a user-centered library. To collect feedback from the users on library services, the Leavey Library and Information Commons staff conducted two formal in-house assessments. In 2003, Leavey librarians undertook a general library survey to assess the quality of library services and to identify any gaps or issues. This survey provided useful data on library users: who they are, why they come to the library, and their level of satisfaction with library services.

In 2004, for the first time, the Leavey Information Commons staff designed and conducted a specialized assessment of Leavey's Commons users. This

survey instrument consisted of twenty-two questions and was administered to the Upper and Lower Commons users over a 24-hour period. The main goal of the assessment was to profile the user community and learn their reasons for using the facility, the library's success in meeting their needs, their level of satisfaction, and finally any suggestions or recommendations for other services or resources. The results of the survey provided an impetus for recent enhancements to resources and services and the initiation of new student spaces in the two Commons.

Other formal campuswide assessments were conducted in 2004 and 2005. LibQUAL+ surveys, conducted in 2004 and 2005, provided a library-wide assessment of library services to USC students, faculty, and staff. The assessment outcome generated data on user satisfaction of the library resources and services. The 2005 Project SAILS assessment targeted undergraduate students in General Education courses, including those enrolled in the Writing Program and related Social Issues and Arts and Letters courses.

In addition, patron feedback/suggestion forms in the Commons and other service locations throughout the library and the "Dear Library" online feedback on the University Libraries' website provide mechanisms for user feedback on Commons and library facilities, staff, services, and resources.

Information Commons Governance

The Information Commons are governed and managed by the Leavey Library staff. The leadership group consists of a librarian and a full-time, professional staff member. The manager is responsible for day-to-day activities of the facilities, supervision of student assistants who work in the Commons, and coordination of troubleshooting issues with the library IT staff. The librarian (information services coordinator) coordinates overall reference and information services activities, handles reference scheduling, designs the training program for the student navigation assistants, and oversees the student assistants' supervision.

Lessons Learned

▌ *Integrated service model.* When Leavey opened in 1994, the initial IC service model involved two separate desks staffed by librarians and student navigation assistants on one side and computer consultants on the other side of the long divided desk. Leavey librarians joined the assistants to assist patrons with informational and research needs, and computer consultants provided in-depth assistance on software issues. Despite the intention for integration of services, there were two separate desks, with two different types of services and minimal communication efforts between the two desks' service providers. Part of the problem related to the fact that computer consultants had no supervision or reporting line to Leavey staff. Their direct supervisor resided in the USC Computing Support Center building. In fall 2000, on the basis of our observations and understanding that many student questions touched on both research and computing areas, Leavey discontinued the computer consultation service agreement with the Computing Support Center and embarked on a truly integrated service model. To further support the integrated service concept, in summer 2005 the Lower Commons desk was redesigned and reconfigured to one piece where librarians, student navigation assistants, and staff sit side by side.

▌ *Collaborative workroom reservation.* The thirty-four group study rooms have been highly popular student space ever since Leavey was established. The reservation process is manual and self-monitored. Because of high demand, students often abuse the reservation process: reservation logs disappear, reservations are crossed out, reservation policy is ignored. This issue requires desk staff to mediate reservation disputes and settle arguments on the reservation policy. Currently, the staff are collaborating with USC Libraries Information Technology consultants to review room reservation software to implement an online reservation system.

▌ *Location of reference collection.* Since the Leavey planners' focus was on technology, librarians were not consulted about the placement of the reference collection. The reference collection lines the walls of the Lower Commons, running two shelves high, to fit under the windows looking into the collaborative workrooms; one wall at the far end of the Commons is all bookshelves. This arrangement stretches the collection out all over the room, which is a disincentive to actual usage. There is a small ready-reference collection behind the reference desk (in the middle of the room), but most of the collection is quite a hike from a busy desk. We have a wide, growing array of e-resources available, so this situation becomes less of an issue each year. The books do add a nice, decorative touch and provide a good contrast to the high-tech workstations. It would, however, work better to have the entire reference collection in one part of the room.

UNIVERSITY OF SOUTHERN MAINE

USM LIBRARIES

Prepared June 2006 by Barbara J. Mann (Coordinator, Information Literacy Program)
and David J. Nutty (Director of Libraries)

Library website	http://library.usm.maine.edu
Carnegie classification	Master's Colleges and Universities (larger programs)
# Undergraduates	8,622
# Graduate students	2,352
# Faculty	399
Highest degree offered	Doctorate
# Volumes	352,325
# Periodical titles	63,801
# FTE librarians	15
# Other FTE staff	24
Library annual budget	$2,968,326 (no separate budget for IC)
Annual circulation	28,426
Annual gate entries	206,600
IC opening date	September 6, 2005
IC name	[campus library] Information Commons
IC service model type	Partially integrated services
# Computer workstations	Portland 15, Gorham 14, Lewiston-Auburn 13
What's on desktop	Internet, proprietary research databases, Microsoft Office suite, subject-specific offerings via computer lab software packages, course management software
IC architect	In-house

Hours	All hours that each library is open:
	    Portland and Gorham: Mon.–Thurs. 8:00 a.m.–11:00 p.m.;
	       Fri. 8:00 a.m.–6:00 p.m.; Sat. 10:00 a.m.–6:00 p.m.;
	       Sun. 10:00 a.m.–10:00 p.m.
	    Lewiston-Auburn: Mon.–Thurs. 8:00 a.m.–8:00 p.m.;
	       Fri. 8:00 a.m.–4:30 p.m.; Sat. 9:00 a.m.–3:00 p.m.; Sun. closed

IC area	Portland 8,694 sq. ft., Gorham 1,665 sq. ft., Lewiston-Auburn 920 sq. ft.
# Physical service points in IC	1 at each of three campuses
Average # IC users in a typical month	Portland 782, Gorham 297, Lewiston-Auburn 212
Print reference materials in the IC?	Yes, each campus library has its own print reference collection.

Location of Institution and Campus Description

The University of Southern Maine has the largest student body of the seven campuses of the University of Maine system, with an enrollment of 10,974 (8,622 undergraduates, 2,352 graduate/law students). USM consists of three campuses: Portland, Gorham (residential campus), and a branch campus in Lewiston-Auburn. USM currently offers forty-seven baccalaureate degrees, twenty-six graduate degrees, and one doctoral program. Each campus has a library, with the Glickman Family Library on the Portland campus serving as the main library. The student body of USM is a mix of generations. There are traditional students, some the first generation to attend college, as well as older students who balance work and family commitments and are either returning to complete their degrees or enrolled for the first time.

Information Commons Description

An information commons has been implemented in all three campus libraries. The Glickman Family Library in Portland is the main campus library. The Glickman Commons is located on the second floor of the library and includes fifteen workstations. Of these fifteen, four are public access machines set up for non-USM researchers and include Microsoft Office. Eight workstations are arranged on a serpentine table, four per side with two more behind this table. All of these workstations feed into a networked laser printer. Four additional workstations sit on an elevated pod and are networked to another smaller laser printer. An adaptive technology workstation is also available on a separate table.

The fourth through seventh floors of the Glickman Library each contain two or three additional workstations per floor. The fifth floor also houses a small computer lab, complete with scanner, and the Center for Information Literacy, an electronic classroom with thirty-six workstations. A laser printer is also available on this floor. All of these computers include the IC software and menu.

The Gorham Campus Library Information Commons has fourteen computers, with ten of these workstations (five each) divided among two computer pods. An L-shaped area contains the other four workstations: two public use machines, one machine dedicated to a special education law software package, and one adaptive technology workstation. The second floor of the library has two additional workstations, which also contain IC software and menu.

The Lewiston-Auburn Campus Library Information Commons features three computer pod areas, one with six workstations, another with five workstations, including an adaptive technology workstation, and an elevated pod for two other workstations.

All three campus libraries provide collaborative workspace in the form of group study rooms or areas as well as individual study areas. The Portland campus also has a media viewing room adjacent to the Commons on the second floor. All three campuses are also wireless environments.

Information Commons Service Transaction Statistics

Statistics are kept at each service point and include directional/research/technical questions asked and whether they are in person or by telephone. One of the goals for the near future is to implement a more robust virtual reference service.

Information Commons Staffing and Training

Research and technical support is provided at each information commons service point, which is also the reference desk. Each desk is staffed singularly from a pool of 9.5 FTE librarians, 3.5 FTE classified staff, and 1 FTE IC student assistant. The number of staff per library varies. The desk in Portland is staffed 67 hours a week, Gorham covers 58 hours a week, and the Lewiston-Auburn campus offers 62.5 hours a week. Because of a small staff, which also provides library instruction and consultation, students are also used to staff the desk, sometimes without librarian backup. At the Portland campus, the IC staff member on duty carries a cell phone and, if he or she steps away from the desk, leaves a sign on the desk alerting the user to this option. The Lewiston-Auburn campus library has a combined Circulation and Information Commons/Reference service desk.

A Blackboard site has been created to serve as training/policy and procedures manual as well as a communication mechanism, especially between staff and students. A full-fledged training procedure is still being drafted. Procedures already in place have been documented and included in the manual.

What's on the Desktop

All USM Information Commons workstations include access, via a branded menu of resources, to the Microsoft Office suite; 194 proprietary databases; EndNote, the bibliographic management software package; Blackboard, course management software; Internet; and the USM Computer Lab software packages. Printing is available on all networked workstations for a fee and requires funds being available on the user's USM card.

Information Commons Assessment

Currently, there are no formalized assessment procedures in place. Goals for the future include the creation of a student advisory board, focus groups, and participation in LibQUAL+. Additionally, software has been added to track workstation log-ins.

Information Commons Governance

An Information Commons Committee oversaw creation of the Information Commons and disbanded after implementation. Decisions are now made by the director of university libraries, head of reference, and Information Commons coordinator, with feedback solicited from all library staff.

Lessons Learned

▍ The urgency to implement the information commons should be tempered by sufficient staff training, especially for student assistants. The idea of traditional reference was more ingrained than expected by staff in all areas of the USM libraries. More standardized and regularized training would have provided a better comfort level with the idea of tiered service. Because we had a cadre of student assistants who were new to providing reference, the need for more and better training became even more apparent.

▍ Staff discussions must be broad-based and repeated. The concept of the information commons was not clearly understood by all staff. Discussions should be continued even after full implementation to create more complete staff buy-in.

▍ Secure sufficient dedicated funding for implementation, particularly to address furniture issues and building additional collaborative spaces.

▍ There is a need for a formalized mechanism for tracking the number of log-ins and length of stay for each user. Although we have anecdotal evidence of increased usage, there are no real statistics.

UNIVERSITY OF VICTORIA

MCPHERSON LIBRARY

Prepared June 2006 by Joanne Henning (Associate University Librarian, Reference and Collection Services)

Library website	http://gateway.uvic.ca
IC website	http://gateway.uvic.ca/ic/index.html
Carnegie classification	Not applicable
# Undergraduates	16,483
# Graduate students	2,423
# Faculty	790
Highest degree offered	Doctorate
# Volumes	1.9 million, 2.2 million microforms, 198,000 cartographic items, 40,000 serial subscriptions, 64,000 sound recordings, 35,000 music scores, 7,900 films and videos, 1,124 linear meters of manuscripts and archival material
# Titles	1.3 million
# Periodical titles	24,680
# FTE librarians	29
# Other FTE staff	109
Library annual budget	C$12,410,352
Annual circulation	382,088
Annual gate entries	436,077
IC opening date	January 2003
IC name	McPherson Library Information Commons
IC service model type	Partially integrated services
# Computer workstations	103
What's on desktop	Internet, subscription databases, word processing, spreadsheet, charting/graphing, desktop publishing, graphics, mathematics/ statistics, multimedia/presentation; details at http://gateway.uvic. ca/ic/pc_software.html
IC architect	Warner James Architects
Hours	Mon.–Thurs. 8:00 a.m.–11:00 p.m.; Fri. 8:00 a.m.–6:00 p.m.; Sat. 10:00 a.m.–6:00 p.m.; Sun. 10:00 a.m.–11:00 p.m.
IC area	25,330 sq. ft.
# Physical service points in IC	3: Loan Desk/Reserve Desk, Reference/Information Commons Assistants Desk, and Map Office
Average # IC users in a typical month	24,230
Print reference materials in the IC?	Yes, the IC includes the reference collection.

Location of Institution and Campus Description

Located in British Columbia, the University of Victoria, one of Canada's leading universities, provides both students and faculty with a unique learning environment. UVic has earned a reputation for commitment to research, scholarship, and co-op education. The university is widely recognized for its innovative and responsive programs and its interdisciplinary and international initiatives. UVic offers outstanding social, cultural, artistic, environmental, and athletic opportunities, including a full schedule of concerts, plays, exhibitions, films, lectures, and athletics events.

Information Commons Description

The McPherson Library Information Commons offers students an opportunity to work in an integrated environment that provides research resources, computing, and reference and instruction services. The Commons offers seventy-five computer workstations in an open area and twenty-eight workstations in the library classroom on the main floor of the library in proximity to the loan desk, reserve desk, and reference desk. Information Commons assistants work from the reference desk to provide technology help to users.

The Information Commons has a variety of comfortable seating spaces on the main floor, numbering 375. Seating includes soft lounge chairs, large tables and chairs, and tablet-arm chairs for use with laptops in the totally wireless environment. It includes ten bookable group study rooms (four on the main floor) and two resource rooms for students with disabilities.

Print collections that are part of the Information Commons include reference, reserve, maps and aerial photos, current periodicals, and newspapers. Additional renovations will bring high-use microforms and music and media to the main floor.

Information Commons Service Transaction Statistics

In 2005/2006 we transacted 26,894 reference questions (reference and directional at the desk, phone, e-mail, and virtual chat) and averaged 4,488 IC assistant questions.

Information Commons Staffing and Training

The Commons is staffed by librarians at the reference desk who provide reference and research assistance and scheduled classes on searching databases, the Internet, and using software such as RefWorks. There may be from one to three librarians on the reference desk during desk hours: Monday–Thursday 9:00 a.m.–9:00 p.m.; Friday 9:00 a.m.–5:00 p.m.; Saturday 11:00 a.m.–5:00 p.m.; and Sunday 11:00 a.m.–9:00 p.m. Virtual reference is offered on a reduced schedule.

The Commons is also staffed by IC assistants, who provide technical support and troubleshooting for technical problems. There is one assistant available from 11:00 a.m. to closing every day of the week.

Practical day-to-day matters, including training, are coordinated by the Public Services Liaison Group, made up of staff from Access and Branch Services and Reference and Collections Services. The liaison group organizes and schedules reference training for IC assistants and technology training for librarians. The aim is to have reference librarians back up the assistants with general support (e.g., printers) and to have the assistants back up the reference librarians with general reference queries (e.g., directional and policy questions, general navigation of the libraries' website, known item searching of the catalogue, finding call numbers).

The IC assistants receive technical training that allows them to troubleshoot basic printer problems, assist with saving and downloading, and troubleshoot equipment booting and rebooting.

What's on the Desktop

Below is a listing of the applications available on the McPherson Library Information Commons computers:

> Accelrys ViewerLite, a molecular visualization tool
>
> Adobe Acrobat and Reader
>
> Beyond 20/20, spreadsheet software to view data produced by Statistics Canada
>
> Cn3D, an application to view 3D structures in a web browser
>
> FTP/Telnet
>
> IMP: Island Medical Program (remote site)
>
> Internet Explorer
>
> IrfanView, software to view images and convert them to other formats
>
> jEdit, a programmer's text editor
>
> Lexis-Nexis
>
> Microsoft Frontpage (not available on all computers)
>
> Microsoft Office suite
>
> Netscape
>
> Quicktime
>
> RealPlayer
>
> RefWorks Write-N-Cite, a reference citing tool that works with word processor applications
>
> Roxio Easy CD Creator
>
> SciFinder Scholar
>
> StuffIt Expander
>
> WebMail, UVic's web-accessible e-mail application
>
> Windows Media Player

Information Commons Assessment

LibQUAL+ was conducted twice; otherwise, no formal assessment has been done on the Information Commons.

Information Commons Governance

The Information Commons is jointly managed by the Access and Branch Services (hire, train, and supervise Information Commons assistants), Reference and Collections Services (provide reference and instruction services), Library IT (provide technical support, both network and desktop), and University Librarian's Office (provide physical space and furniture). All library partners sit on the Information Commons Steering Committee, where planning and problem solving take place.

Lessons Learned

▌ The Information Commons should have been networked from the start.

▌ We need a timely way to make decisions regarding requests for peripherals, additional software, and the like.

▌ We need a plan for equipment upgrade. Because the Commons evolved, the newer machines always went to the newer areas, leaving the classroom (the first Commons development) with the oldest equipment.

▌ Plan for queuing.

Mixed seating within the IC (Abilene Christian University; used by permission of PURE Photography and Abilene Christian University Library)

Writing Center partner in the IC (Abilene Christian University; used by permission of PURE Photography and Abilene Christian University Library)

Procrastination Station Café (University of Massachusetts, Amherst; photo by Anne Moore)

Express computer workstations within the IC (Abilene Christian University; used by permission of PURE Photography and Abilene Christian University Library)

IC café (Abilene Christian University; used by permission of PURE Photography and Abilene Christian University Library)

Serpentine computer workstation tables (University of Calgary;
photo by Guy Polak, courtesy of University of Calgary)

Collaborative computer workstations with privacy sails
(SUNY Binghamton; used by permission)

Soft seating buffers computer workstation areas in the IC (Indiana University, Bloomington; photo by Joanne Henning)

Group study area within the IC (Indiana University, Bloomington; courtesy of Indiana University Libraries)

IC atrium provides natural lighting (University of North Carolina, Charlotte; author photo)

Express computer workstations (Rhode Island School of Design; author photo)

Glass-enclosed group study rooms (University of Missouri, Kansas City; photo by Joanne Henning)

IC computer workstation privacy partitions (University of Southern California; courtesy of University of Southern California Libraries)

Information station service desk with dual monitors for patron participation (Providence College; courtesy of Providence College)

Cell Zone booth helps keep noise down (University of Massachusetts, Amherst; photo by Anne Moore)

Office supplies vending machine in the IC (University of Massachusetts, Amherst; photo by Anne Moore)

Beanbag seating in IC group study rooms (Rhode Island School of Design; author photo)

Individual computer workstation (SUNY Binghamton; used by permission)

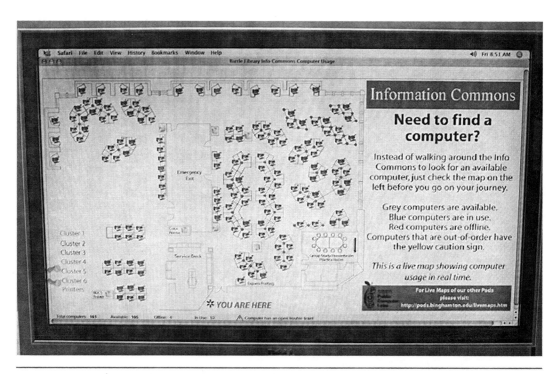

Computer availability map showing which public computers are being used
and which are available (SUNY Binghamton; used by permission)

## chapter seven

Information Commons Case Studies: Small Academic Libraries

ABILENE CHRISTIAN UNIVERSITY

MARGARET AND HERMAN BROWN LIBRARY

Prepared June 2006 by John Mark Tucker, Ph.D.
(Dean of Library and Information Services) and
Mark McCallon, Ph.D. (Assistant Director)

Location of Institution and Campus Description

Founded in Abilene, Texas, in 1906 as Childers Classical Institute, we became Abilene Christian College in 1920 and Abilene Christian University in 1976. ACU enrolls 4,200 students in sixty baccalaureate programs and 600 graduate students in twenty-seven master's programs and one doctoral program. Students and alumni, more than 86,000, represent fifty states and 109 nations. With a student-teacher ratio of 17 to 1, ACU routinely ranks in the top twenty among 126 private colleges west of the Mississippi River.

The campus was on North First Street until 1929, when it was moved to the northeast section of the city. ACU is on a 208-acre campus approximately 180 miles west of the Dallas/Fort Worth area.

Library website	http://www.acu.edu/library/
IC website	http://www.acu.edu/library/learningcommons/
Carnegie classification	Master's Colleges and Universities (medium programs)
# Undergraduates	4,200
# Graduate students	600
# Faculty	225
Highest degree offered	Doctorate
# Volumes	507,000 at ACU, 1.5 million in Abilene Library Consortium
# Periodical titles	2,300 print journals exclusive of online titles
# FTE librarians	10
# Other FTE staff	13
Library annual budget	$1,450,000
Annual circulation	57,500
Annual gate entries	300,000 before IC opening
IC opening date	2006
IC name	Abilene Christian University Learning Commons
IC service model type	Partially integrated services
# Computer workstations	71 including circulating laptops
What's on desktop	Internet, proprietary research databases, office suites, word processing, spreadsheet, charting/graphing, graphics, multimedia/presentation
IC architect	Tittle Luther Partnership, Abilene, Texas
Hours	All hours the library is open: Mon., Tues., Thurs. 7:00 a.m.–12:00 a.m.; Wed. 7:00 a.m.–6:00 p.m., 8:30 p.m.–12:00 a.m.; Fri. 7:00 a.m.–5:00 p.m.; Sat. 9:00 a.m.–6:00 p.m.; Sun. 1:00 p.m.–5:00 p.m., 7:00 p.m.–12:00 a.m.
IC area	14,450 sq. ft. in library; 25,000 sq. ft. including Center for Teaching and Learning and campus telecommunication and networking
# Physical service points in IC	7
Average # IC users in a typical month	42,000 projected on the basis of initial weekly attendance
Print reference materials in the IC?	Yes, the main print reference book collection is in the research area of the IC.

Information Commons Description

The ACU Learning Commons area is 14,450 square feet of prime real estate in a major building—the Brown Library—on the west side of the university mall. The Learning Commons shares a foyer with the Adams Center for Teaching and Learning and the Technology Help Desk (for staff and faculty), both of which are Learning Commons partners and have been involved since the earliest stages of exploration, brainstorming, and planning.

The Learning Commons provides the entry into the Margaret and Herman Brown Library. We adopted a mall concept with principal services readily visible from most perspectives on the main floor. The Learning Commons features the Adams Center, art galleries, café service, collaborative workspaces, lounge-type seating, photocopy services plus technology support, information literacy and instructional services, library circulation, research assistance, and the Writing Center and Speaking Center.

The Adams Center for Teaching and Learning installs, maintains, and upgrades departmental computer labs and smart classrooms. The Center also concentrates on faculty development and enrichment to promote effective uses of technology in classroom settings.

Art galleries include exhibit spaces for rotating collections of student and faculty art. The café service, operated by ARAMARK, is a full-service Starbucks, offering coffee products, sandwiches, salads, and soup.

Collaborative workspaces constitute the focal point of the Learning Commons. One of our surveys showed that 96 percent of ACU professors create assignments for students to work in teams. Twenty-four computer workstations are arranged on custom-made, U-shaped tables that easily accommodate five or six students engaged in group study projects. Lightweight, oval tables create a dynamic atmosphere that encourages students to devise their own workspaces. The Learning Commons has become the technology-rich environment where students can become fully engaged in collaborative academic projects.

The Copy Center provides multimedia development; image and text scanning; monochrome, color, and large-format printing for business documents and reports; and binding and finishing services. The center also rents digital video and digital still cameras at a nominal cost.

Information literacy and instructional services have become available in a wide range of settings and feature the library research component of University 100, a course required of all freshmen. The library faculty has created and continues to enhance an online tutorial, conducts course-related instruction, and collaborates with the Adams Center on workshops for faculty, staff, and students. These services preceded the construction of the Learning Commons by several years.

Library circulation provides traditional circulation, reserve, and document delivery functions and also participates in a daily courier service for the 1.5 million volumes in member libraries of the Abilene Library Consortium: ACU, Abilene Public Library, Hardin-Simmons University, Howard Payne University, and McMurry University.

Library Research Assistance features reference and research guidance using print and online databases including the Abilene Library Consortium catalog. Staffed by library faculty, this service also facilitates interlibrary loan transactions, information services for the library's U.S. Government Publications Depository, and close consultation with the Writing Center and Team 55 for students preparing research-intensive papers and class presentations. Team 55 is the campuswide service for student computing. It assists with network and account setups, conducts computer diagnostics and repair, troubleshoots virus and spyware problems, and directs Copy Center services. Team 55 also maintains laptop computers for short-term loan to students, faculty, and staff in the building.

The Technology Help Desk provides data networking and telecommunication services for the entire campus, computer support for staff and faculty, and oversight of Team 55 (student computing support).

The Writing Center, directed by the Department of English, assists students in all disciplines with ideas for writing, revising, and editing drafts, preparing resumes and cover letters, documenting, and formatting. The Center makes referrals to Library Research Assistance when supporting information becomes essential for high-quality term papers. The Writing Center also shares staff with the Department of Communication for scheduling use of the Speaking Center, a lab located in another building that helps students with effective delivery of oral presentations.

Information Commons Service Transaction Statistics

Little information is available since our installation opened in April 2006. Early projections indicate that gate count is up 60 percent; Writing Center use increased 35 percent; Library Research (reference) Assistance increased 20 percent; and book circulation increased slightly.

Information Commons Staffing and Training

The Learning Commons partners are keenly aware that we are merging cultures with different vocabularies, value systems, and service models. We have held meetings with all service providers including students, a total of 125 individuals. We distributed an employee handbook that describes our mission, values, and expectations as well as protocols for internal and external communication.

Regular partner meetings and close physical proximity have facilitated the merging of cultures and the creation of the new Learning Commons culture. All participants seem quite sensitive to the difficulties involved in developing a common language and in teaching ourselves to cooperate in new ways. We are very much a work-in-progress.

What's on the Desktop

All computer workstations in the Learning Commons allow access to productivity software (Microsoft Office, charting/graphing, mathematics/statistics,

multimedia/presentation) as well as to the library's proprietary databases and the Internet. The workstations are identical to those in campus labs. Two kiosk workstations with Internet access, databases, and selected productivity applications (Microsoft Word, Excel, and PowerPoint) serve guests of the university. All workstations have DVD and CD playback capabilities.

Five high-end iMac workstations are available with Final Cut Express and the iLife '06 suite (iMovie, iPhoto, iDVD). Two of these have scanners attached and three have VCRs available for movie editing.

Information Commons Assessment

We assess the library instructional component of University 100, a course required of all freshmen, through an interactive online tutorial that includes pre-test and post-test assessment. We also include library questions regarding personnel, services, and collections on the junior class survey.

For the ACU Learning Commons, teams of architecture and interior design students conducted needs assessments about the library, and two groups of students in the College of Business Administration conducted market research among faculty and students.

Our next step will involve outcomes assessments conducted by a staff team from Educational Technology, the Office of Institutional Research and Assessment, and the ACU Library.

Information Commons Governance

Departments at ACU operate on a five-year plan, a narrative that is updated annually and provides the basis for budget proposals. The Learning Commons partners integrated the needs and interests of the Commons into the five-year plans of their respective units for the first time in the budget cycle for 2005/2006.

The partners contribute staff to each of the major services of the Learning Commons. The partners report, through their varying departments, to the provost except for the café service, which reports to administrative services. They meet about twice a month and distribute minutes of their meetings. On another level, those of us who plan and implement the Learning Commons work in close proximity and engage in problem solving on a daily basis.

Lessons Learned

▮ We learned to keep an open mind. We did not assume that decades of formal education, as well as reading, writing, attending conferences, and serving in libraries, had provided us with all the answers for best practices. We questioned long-held assumptions and shot sacred cows.

▮ We listened to students. We watched them work, studied them, learned about them. We read the literature of higher education and learning styles and became conversant with the ways that students communicate, socialize, and multitask.

▮ We expanded partnerships beyond faculty. Although faculty members remained our most critically important partners, many other staff members played key roles. These included contractors, the English Department, Art Department, and food and housekeeping services. They also included, obviously, educational technology specialists who have become increasingly important over the past several years. We sought a definition for the Learning Commons that goes beyond merely displacing reference books and installing computers. We established relationships—genuine partnerships—that will help expand the library's resourcefulness and influence on campus life.

ASBURY THEOLOGICAL SEMINARY

B. L. FISHER LIBRARY

Prepared June 2006 by Kenneth A. Boyd, Ph.D. (Dean of Information Services)

Library and IC website	http://www.asburyseminary.edu/information/
Carnegie classification	Special focus institutions—theological seminaries
# Undergraduates	0
# Graduate students	1,700
# Faculty	60 full-time, 126 part-time
Highest degree offered	Doctorate
# Volumes	415,000
# Periodical titles	1,100
# FTE librarians	8 IC, 8 Technical Services/IT
# Other FTE staff	8 full-time and 2 part-time IC, 10 Technical Services/IT
Library annual budget	$2,500,000
Annual circulation	100,000
IC opening date	August 1, 2003
IC name	Information Commons
IC service model type	Primarily integrated services
# Computer workstations	85, including Macintosh stations
What's on desktop	Internet, proprietary research databases, office suites, word processing, multimedia/presentation, BibleWorks
IC architect	Local design committee
Hours	All hours the library is open: Mon.–Thurs. 7:30 a.m.–12:00 a.m.; Fri. 7:30 a.m.–6:00 p.m.; Sat. 8:00 a.m.–6:00 p.m.; Sun. closed
IC area	34,630 sq. ft.
# Physical service points in IC	1 for students in Kentucky, 1 for students in Florida, and 1 for all faculty in Kentucky
Print reference materials in the IC?	Yes

Location of Institution and Campus Description

Asbury Theological Seminary was founded in 1923 and named after Francis Asbury, America's first Methodist bishop. Asbury Seminary is a multi-denominational graduate school of theology committed to teaching in the historic Wesleyan tradition. Total enrollment is more than 1,700, with students coming from eighty-six different denominations and forty-two countries. Asbury's main campus is in Wilmore, Kentucky, just south of Lexington. Known for its use of technology in theological education, Asbury Seminary established a virtual campus, Extended Learning (ExL), in 1997. Further expansion occurred two years later in 1999, when Asbury opened a campus in Orlando, Florida.

Information Commons Description

The Information Commons encompasses the entire library building, which was built in 1967. The Commons was created in 2003 when circulation, reference, and computer support were integrated into one service desk. This integration has created a "one-stop shop" for our students. Whether students have a problem finding a book or their computer has crashed, they can come to the Information Commons desk for help. The combination of service points has also enabled us to provide extended service hours.

By merging library and information technology services, we facilitated student learning with the addition of an adaptive technology center, video editing bays, quick-stop walk-up stations, student collaboration rooms, wireless access, and just-in-time training computers.

Many types of learning environments have been created, ranging from group to personal study space. Students can choose from comfortable leather lounge chairs, individual study carrels, or tables. They can choose from a quiet study area, a collaboration area, or a coffee-shop atmosphere. During warmer weather an outside porch with wireless access is available.

Integrated information technology and the library website provide online databases, resources, and tutorials for students. This same integration also brought about technology equipment checkouts, which include laptops, video cameras, digital cameras, tripods, audiocassette recorders/players, microphones, headphones, flash drives, VGA cables, Ethernet cables, audiovisual cables, and video projectors. In 2006, checkouts for all students were extended to six months.

The same IC model has been applied to our Florida campus.

Traditional library technical services and information technology, although part of information services, is located in another building and not in the Information Commons.

Information Commons Service Transaction Statistics

With the integration of circulation, reference, and technology, the traditional reference statistics were discontinued. Since the Information Commons was initiated, 870 computers have been configured for wireless access, and there have been more than 16,000 e-mail transactions for IC services (library loan, audiovisual duplication, computer support, advanced research, distance learning support).

Information Commons Staffing and Training

The Information Commons has six professional staff with library degrees, graduate degrees, or specialized training. Seven full-time staff and two part-time staff provide support for the professional staff. All staff have an area of specialization and are cross-trained to provide initial support for both library and computer questions. Generally, two people are scheduled at the IC desk. To provide further support there are twelve student workers. In addition to the staff listed above, there are two professionals and one support position in the Florida campus Information Commons.

Support staff are encouraged to pursue professional training, normally the M.L.S. degree. A raise is given if they start the program, and three years are allowed to complete the program. Upon completion of the degree they are given another raise. In the future, the seminary will pay for support staff classes toward the M.L.S. degree or other appropriate courses. One example might be in the area of instructional design.

On-the-job training is provided through a program developed by our IC managers. Training includes workshops on both technology and library-related topics. Biweekly reference questions are given to the full-time staff to provide training in basic library resources.

There are eight professional staff and ten support staff in library technical services and information technology that are not located in the Information Commons.

What's on the Desktop

Campus e-mail/Collaborative Classroom System

Information Commons Homepage—Active Desktop

BibleWorks 6.0

Mozilla, Firefox, and Internet Explorer

Microsoft Office, Mozilla Composer, and Final Cut Pro

Information Commons Assessment

The Information Commons is evaluated by an ongoing seminary assessment program and a graduating student survey. Staff have annual professional appraisals/evaluations that include self-evaluation.

Information Commons Governance

The Information Commons is part of Information Services and is supervised by the dean of Information Services. The dean reports to the vice president for academic affairs and is a member of the Academic Council and the President's Leadership Team.

Lessons Learned

▌ The environment of the Information Commons is dynamic and always changing. Continued growth is necessary to maintain relevance and progress. We cannot afford to become complacent or feel like we have "arrived."

▌ There is a responsibility to provide varied learning environments to meet the needs of different learning styles. This can take the form of individual carrels, collaborative workstations, group study rooms, comfortable lounge chairs, tables for study, quiet study areas, and noisy study areas.

▌ Standardization and simplification of policies make it easier to train staff and acquaint users with policies.

CARLETON COLLEGE

LAURENCE MCKINLEY GOULD LIBRARY

Prepared June 2006 by Carolyn Sanford (Head of Reference and Instruction) with assistance
from Andrea Nixon (Assistant Director of Academic Computing), Heather Tompkins (Research/IT Librarian),
and Troy Barkmeier (Student Computing Coordinator)

Library website	http://apps.carleton.edu/campus/library/
IC website	http://apps.carleton.edu/campus/its/
Carnegie classification	Baccalaureate Colleges—Arts & Sciences
# Undergraduates	1,932
# Faculty	182
Highest degree offered	Baccalaureate
# Volumes	913,330
# Titles	645,230
# Periodical titles	1,551 print, 12,884 electronic
# FTE librarians	13
# Other FTE staff	15
Library annual budget	$3,500,000
Annual circulation	67,857
Annual gate entries	286,084
IC opening date	September 2004
IC name	Reference Room
IC service model type	Partially integrated services
# Computer workstations	26 PCs and Macintoshes
What's on desktop	Internet, proprietary research databases, office suites, word processing, EndNote, spreadsheet, charting/graphing, desktop publishing, graphics, mathematics/statistics, multimedia/ presentation
IC architect	Meyer, Scherer & Rockcastle (architects); Shepley Bulfinch Richardson & Abbott (consulting architects)
Hours	Most hours the library is open
IC area	8,842 sq. ft.
# Physical service points in IC	1
Average # IC users in a typical month	ca. 2,650
Print reference materials in the IC?	Yes, 11,538 volumes (5,881 titles)

Location of Institution and Campus Description

Carleton College, a private four-year liberal arts college founded in 1866, is 40 miles south of Minneapolis-St. Paul, Minnesota, in the small town of Northfield. Approximately 1,900 students who hail from all over the United States and about twenty-seven other countries come to this highly selective college to study. With a student-faculty ratio of 9 to 1, students get to know the faculty and may collaborate with them on their research. Special features of the campus include an exceptional Japanese garden and an 800-acre arboretum with many restored prairie areas. There are 1.9 Frisbees per capita and more than 21,000 cookies baked and consumed by students annually at the Dacie Moses house. The culture reflects a serious scholarly focus along with what has been described as a "quirky" approach to campus life.

Information Commons Description

The library at Carleton is a lovely building that has provided wonderful space since an addition and renovation in 1984. It is spacious and airy with views through many large windows. On entering the atrium, library patrons have a narrow view back to our information commons. At the request of the faculty, we have retained the name Reference Room. Heading back to this north end of the building, people pass the Rookery, a newly designed quiet reading space with a mix of tables, couches, and soft chairs—a small living room space that contains art exhibits, current newspapers, new books, a children's book collection, paperbacks, and popular print periodicals.

As patrons enter the 8,842-square-foot Reference Room, they suddenly find themselves in a spacious room with wall-length large windows to the ceiling on the north and east sides. For the first time since the library was built in 1954, the tall shelving has been replaced with lower shelving, opening up the view to the small lake and the arboretum. Because this one change respected the architectural integrity of the room, it is dramatic and people are stunned to see the difference the low shelving makes in opening up the whole room. This shelving invites more browsing and provides opportunities for seeing librarians and students using the reference collection, either together or individually.

Along the south wall is the computer area, where twenty-one computers are available on various-sized tables arranged in several patterns. The goal was to provide larger tables for students wanting room to spread out their materials or to work with partners. These tables can be reconfigured into different groupings. Since the room has wireless capability, students often use their laptops when working in groups or at the noncomputer tables. Even the long bank of eight computers allows two to three students to work together. Students can easily move the colorful green or blue vinyl mesh chairs with coasters to where they need to work or socialize. There are two printers, two scanners, and a mix of PCs and Macintoshes. Many of these changes reflect our interest in using this space as a prototype as we think about a library addition.

The footprint of the reference shelves provides a division between the computer area and the tables used for large group, small group, or individual studying along the north and east sides. The traditional library tables along the windows had worked well before and were too popular to change. They still provide favorite spaces for individuals, friends, or small groups to study either with their laptop plugged in or just with their readings or problem sets. Lamps were added on these tables to provide better lightning and make a more inviting area, especially in the evening. The layout of the room allows spaces for large group study tables as islands among the shelves.

Reference liaison librarian offices are along the west wall, visible and accessible for individual appointments. Tucked into a nearby open space is the Drawing Board corner, where a 50-inch plasma screen and SMART Board with wireless keyboard and mouse are available. The furniture consists of a U-shaped group of couches with attached low dividers. Up to eight students can work here on projects, practice presentations, or just have a group discussion. Small classes, students, or staff may schedule a session in this space. More computer capacity is available in the library instruction lab completed in 2003 (fifteen PCs) and a new Mac lab with fifteen computers one floor below the Reference Room.

Implemented in the fall of 2004, the Research/ IT service (pronounced "research it") provides a more convenient and integrated service for the students and aids in collaboration between the Gould Library and Information Technology Services (ITS). The renovation offered the opportunity for implementation of a joint computer help/reference desk. The ITS/Library Joint Planning Committee developed a service grid that helped each department understand the goals and objectives for the service. Important aspects of the new service include these:

Student Computing Information Center (SCIC) worker provides software assistance and troubleshoots equipment problems and log-in issues.

Reference librarians are freed up to spend more time helping students with research.

New technology supports research using large data sets, GIS, and future research trends.

Students are able to produce papers, presentations, and multimedia projects in the same setting where they conduct their research.

Other changes in the area or associated with reference services include the Silver Screen area one floor below the Reference Room, a small group space consisting of a computer workstation with Sympodium software that functions like a SMART Board but projects onto a glass screen; a whiteboard with news at the Research/IT desk that is archived in the whiteboard blog; and GIS software and data sets available on three computers.

Information Commons Service Transaction Statistics

The Reference Room is a high-traffic location insofar as it is the campus computing lab with the largest number of daily log-ins on campus. With the redesign of this space, room use rose significantly to an average of 2,700 students per month. As a part of updating our services, we implemented a subject liaison model that has been very successful. Our individual appointments combined with in-depth e-mail reference with students increased from about 150 interactions several years ago up to 600 interactions in 2004/2005.

Information Commons Staffing and Training

The Research/IT desk provides a more complete service point for students by offering the expertise of the librarian and the troubleshooting knowledge of the student IT worker. When possible, every SCIC worker has at least one shift in the library, establishing a culture that the Research/IT desk is as important as the original service point in the IT building. Reference librarians staff the desk 54 hours a week, and students cover the same hours as the SCIC desk in the computing center building—100 hours a week. Frequent interaction between the SCIC students and librarians has resulted in the sharing of expertise and closer collaborations.

The designated Research/IT librarian works closely with the SCIC staff coordinator and the library technology librarian on training, technology, scheduling issues, and new ideas. Their close collaboration provides the key to the success of the new service. All SCIC student workers receive handbooks and training from both the ITS and the library staff. After the first year, the original training program was expanded in depth and breadth. The SCIC wiki created a knowledge base for sharing updates and problem-solving tips. Both students and librarians add to the wiki. Categories include facilities, software, operating systems, hardware, connectivity, malware, printing, and e-mail.

What's on the Desktop

All public lab computers in the library, including those in the Reference Room, have a full complement of software available on campus that constitutes our standard academic toolset. This includes productivity tools, document viewers, database tools for working with bibliographic records and image collections, statistical packages, geographic information systems, and an array of discipline-specific applications. Included in the toolset are Acrobat, ArtStor, Can8, Chem Draw, EndNote (campus site license), EZ CD Creator, Firefox, Grammatica, iTunes, Mathematica, Microsoft Office, Mulberry, Neurons in Action, Flash, Java, Picasa, Real, scanner software, SciFinder, SPSS, SSH, and Windows Media Player. Two networked printers are in the Reference Room, and there are additional printers in each of the two third-floor labs. One color printer is available.

Information Commons Assessment

Interviews and surveys, along with feedback from librarians and general student comments, have provided the library with some evaluative information. We also note on our room statistics if students are studying in a group or using a laptop. This gives us some numbers that back up our observations that the larger computer tables are used by students to spread out their materials and for group work. Although the students always mention the couches as wonderful additions, the tables and computers are often in use. Since the room is usually packed with students, we have not worried about success but about managing the space and services effectively.

Information Commons Governance

The library director and the ITS director, both of whom report to the dean of the college, meet weekly. The assistant director of academic computing and the head of reference join them on a regular schedule to discuss issues of mutual concern, including the Reference Room, labs in the library, and joint projects. The coordinator of student computing and others attend the meeting when appropriate. The designated Research/IT librarian meets weekly with the Student Computing Information Center Help Desk coordinator and the library technology coordinator to discuss ideas and issues, plan training, and resolve problems.

Lessons Learned

▌ Communication turned out to be the most important aspect of the project. At times communication failed with people responsible for project, design, or construction.

▌ Be open-minded about recommendations and designs, but trust your knowledge about your own library and the ways it is used or will need to be used.

▌ Recognize that it is difficult for many people to visualize a new layout, leading them to reject changes initially. It is vital to not only find ways to help staff and other campus constituencies understand why there are changes but also provide multiple ways to visualize those changes.

CHAMPLAIN COLLEGE

MILLER INFORMATION COMMONS

Prepared June 2006 by Sarah F. Cohen (Technical Librarian) and
Janet R. Cottrell (Director of Academic Resources and the Library)

Library and IC website	http://campus.champlain.edu/mic/
Carnegie classification	Baccalaureate Colleges—Diverse Fields
# Undergraduates	1,704 full-time
# Graduate students	66 (fall 2005)
# Faculty	66 full-time, 207 part-time
Highest degree offered	Master's
# Volumes	40,380 (excludes e-books and print serials)
# Titles	70,690 (includes e-books)
# Periodical titles	190 print, 20,455 full-text e-journals
# FTE librarians	3.92
# Other FTE Staff	2.7
Annual circulation	5,224
Annual gate entries	139,489 (2004/2005)
IC opening date	April 30, 1998
IC name	Robert E. and Holly D. Miller Information Commons
IC service model type	Partially integrated services
# Computer workstations	54 stations and 4 lendable laptops
What's on desktop	45 general use computers: Internet, proprietary research databases, Microsoft Office suite, and extensive departmental support software.
IC architect	Truex, Cullins & Partners Architects (Note: winners of the Hertzel Pasackow Award for significant contributions to the physical or architectural quality of downtown Burlington for their design)
Hours	Mon.–Thurs. 7:30 a.m.–12:00 a.m.; Fri. 7:30 a.m.–10:00 p.m.; Sat. 10:00 a.m.–10:00 p.m.; Sun. 10:00 a.m.–12:00 a.m.
IC area	24,000 sq. ft.
# Physical service points in IC	5
Average # IC users in a typical month	= gate entries (see above)
Print reference materials in the IC?	Yes, 3,707 volumes housed in IC.

Location of Institution and Campus Description

Champlain College is located in the historic, residential Hill Section neighborhood in the heart of Burlington, Vermont. The campus's facilities integrate the area's historic architecture with the modern, seen in the Victorian-style mansions used as student housing and the stylistically compatible modern buildings that honor Vermont's architectural history of red brick, shingle, slate, and natural light. The Miller Information Commons typifies this combination.

Founded in 1878, Champlain College is a four-year, bachelor's and master's degree granting institution. With 1,704 full-time students and a student-faculty ratio of 17 to 1, Champlain is focused on professional preparation, coupled with a coordinated liberal arts core that integrates technology and focuses on critical thinking and communication skills.

Information Commons Description

Inside the entrance of the Miller Information Commons, the two-floor atrium gives the interior an open, inviting character. Patrons are welcomed by student workers from the circulation desk, offering assistance and direction. Students on the desk are trained to direct patrons to a reference librarian on duty or in a nearby office, give basic reference assistance, direct patrons to other offices or labs in the Commons, and provide general information assistance. Students at the circulation desk also report technical difficulties to the IT help desk and provide basic security monitoring. The circulation desk, which acts as the focal point of the floor, also acts as a repository for campus information and publications.

The main level of Miller Information Commons includes the circulation desk (and reference station), nine reference computers, the print reference collection, librarians' offices, a reading room, print periodicals, the microform and audiovisual viewing room, a copier room, and study tables and chairs.

The second floor of the Commons houses one of the campus computer labs with networked printer. Student assistants offer basic technical assistance for the forty-five computers on this and the ground and third floors. These students also check and maintain the four network printers in the building. Network jacks are also available in the tower reading room and along numerous study spaces. The second floor also houses faculty offices and the Writing Lab as well as the CORE Learning Center for faculty.

The third floor is the main study floor of the Commons. Two large study tables look out to Lake Champlain, with additional terrace seating available seasonally. Oversized chairs line the walls and windows of the third floor as well as the two study nooks. The Vista Room provides one of Burlington's most illustrious views and is often used for meetings and receptions. The East/West Conference Rooms also provide meeting spaces but can also be used for special exhibits such as Champlain College's showing of the national traveling exhibit "Alexander Hamilton, the Man Who Made Modern America." Group study rooms, equipped with network jacks and whiteboards, are available on the third and second floors. The electronic classroom provides thirty recessed computers that can be controlled from the podium as well as from the desk. The podium also has remote controls for slide, video, and multimedia presentations. The third floor also houses the children's literature collection and additional resource materials for the college's early and secondary education majors.

The ground floor of the Commons houses the library's bookstacks as well as three general use computers, individual study rooms, Technical Services, and a second electronic classroom. The ground floor also accommodates the college's Computer Network Center, a temperature-controlled, humidity-specific server room.

Information Commons Service Transaction Statistics

The number of reference questions encountered by professional librarians is recorded. In 2004/2005, librarians served 711 questions. As of May 1, 2006, reference questions for the 2005/2006 academic year were up to 989, showing an increase of 39 percent. The nature of the questions is also tracked and shows an increase in substantive questions rather than directional. These reference statistics do not reflect questions addressed by student workers when working at either the circulation desk or computer help desk.

Library instruction sessions in the classroom rose from thirty-five sessions in 2003/2004 to fifty-five sessions in 2004/2005. The number of students reached in the sessions increased accordingly, from 632 to 1,127 students.

Information Commons Staffing and Training

Miller Information Commons is open and staffed 106.5 hours per week, with only 3.92 FTE librarians and 2.7 FTE staff. The Commons staff pride themselves on accomplishing so much with so few. All librarians participate in reference shifts throughout the day. Three librarians also work at the reference desk in the evenings, offering students and evening faculty assistance until 9:00 p.m. Nametags identify librarians, staff, and student workers to patrons.

Student workers receive training and consistent, extensive review of their duties from the circulation manager. Students and library circulation assistants are given individual training sheets that indicate areas of training covered. On-the-job training and shadowing of existing workers are essential. Student workers receive weekly quizzes ranging in topics from circulation parameters to interlibrary loan procedures. Students are trained on shelving techniques using Library of Congress classification through an interactive computer program called LC-Easy. As students learn the LC system, their work is reviewed by the circulation coordinator. Upon successful completion of training, students are incrementally employed in shelving.

Students who have successfully completed training and continue to work for the Commons past one semester are required to work one hour a week "off the desk" shelf reading. Students are trained individually on how to read call numbers throughout the range and understand the flow of shelves, and they are given tracking sheets for review by the circulation assistants. When students find shelving mistakes, rather than immediately correcting them, they place the misshelved item spine down on the shelf, enabling their supervisor to see what the students consider a mistake. This has made a significant difference in correcting misplaced materials but, more important, it demonstrates and secures student workers' understanding of the order of books on a shelf.

Circulation assistants, who man the library 64 hours a week, of which 44 hours are without librarians present (nights and weekends), are trained individually by the circulation manager. They are given in-depth training on all students' responsibilities and participate in the same quizzes that have effectively trained students. They are also trained on more advanced integrated library system processes such as adding items on the fly, adding messages to patron accounts, and overriding specific system parameters such as lending reference materials to faculty. The majority of their training is based on on-the-job experience. The circulation manager encourages assistants to contact her via e-mail or by phone with any questions or concerns. They are also encouraged to participate with librarians in dealing with issues that arise and develop their own interests in librarianship. For example, recently two of the four circulation assistants participated in a basic reference course offered online that was fully funded by the Commons. Librarians are strongly encouraged to continue their education through training, conferences, institutes, and classes.

What's on the Desktop

The forty-five general use computers offer the Microsoft Office suite, including Visio, Project, and Publisher; Internet access; Adobe Acrobat Reader; Nero Suite; ScriptWorks; Winzip; and GlubTech Secure FTP. Computers are also equipped with Kurzweil 3000 to assist visually impaired and learning disabled students. These computers also include programs to support most majors.

Reference computers on the main level of the Miller Information Commons do not include the Microsoft Office suite and are intended for reference use rather than general use. Reference computers are equipped with Internet access to all library proprietary databases. Free printing is available on all networked computers.

Information Commons Assessment

Champlain College recently went through NEASC reaccredidation, with the library's participation in Standard 7 (Library and Information Resources) of the NEASC standards.

Miller Information Commons completed its LibQUAL+ survey in spring 2005. As a result of the survey, focus groups with different constituents (traditional age students, commuting students, faculty) have been conducted to better identify ways the library and the Commons can improve. In spring 2006, the library conducted its departmental self-review (required by the Champlain College Institutional Self-Assessment Cycle), which included comparisons based on data collected from a group of colleges identified as peer institutions.

Reference statistics are gathered throughout the year and all library instruction sessions conclude with distribution of a feedback survey to all participating students.

Information Commons Governance

Unlike most institutions, at Champlain the Information Commons houses the library. The director of academic resources reports directly to the provost. Four faculty members act in an advisory capacity to the director.

Lessons Learned

▌ Aesthetics matter. Creating a space that people want to come into is a necessary and worthwhile goal. Through careful siting both on the campus

and in the neighborhood, extraordinary architecture that reflects and reinterprets the design of stately homes in the area, and comfortable interior styling, Miller Information Commons is widely acknowledged as a beautiful building. With its striking exterior, warm and welcoming interior, many windows, and view of Lake Champlain from the top floor, the Commons is often recognized as one of the nicest buildings in the city, and one that students, faculty, staff, and visitors like to walk into. This translates into a consistently high gate count and frees us from concern about whether students will continue to come to the library as online resources—and other beautiful campus buildings—proliferate. In short, "We built it, and they came."

▌ The concept of an information commons may be hard to define, but it works, and it can even be surprisingly elastic. Colocating library resources and services with computing labs, a writing center, a teaching and learning center, and other features—in whatever mix—seems to make sense to faculty and students. Over the years, the mix in Miller Information Commons has changed considerably. For example, when another new building opened on campus several years after the Commons opened, the high-end multimedia labs originally housed in the Commons moved there as part of a new graphics and design area. Students and faculty adjusted well to the change, and the Commons gate count continued to increase in spite of the relocation of this major service area. Similarly, in 2005 some faculty offices moved in and the new CORE teaching and learning center opened in the Commons—again, faculty and students accepted these changes easily.

▌ Some unique design features can be both constraining and liberating. As part of the 1990s excitement over the growing use of online databases and the advent of electronic books, the Commons was designed to house a print collection of only 60,000 volumes—a severe restriction for any academic library. But this constraint also frees us from having to address other difficult issues such as those surrounding storage of bound journal collections (we have none; there simply isn't space). We are forced to keep our print book collection vibrant and relevant and have adopted a rallying cry of "Make Every Book Count." The challenge of providing a strong collection in such limited space has provided a wonderful opportunity for collaboration with our faculty and brings them not just into the Commons but into the stacks for regular evaluation, weeding, and collection development efforts. It also fosters ongoing creativity as we try to find new ways to use our space effectively.

DICKINSON COLLEGE

WAIDNER-SPAHR LIBRARY

Prepared June 2006 by Robert E. Renaud
(Vice President and CIO, Library and Information Services)

Library website	http://lis.dickinson.edu/Library/
IC website	http://lis.dickinson.edu/Technology/Public%20Labs/ Information%20Commons/index.html
Carnegie classification	Baccalaureate Colleges—Arts & Sciences
# Undergraduates	2,255
# Graduate students	0
# Faculty	209
Highest degree offered	Baccalaureate
# Volumes	520,449
# Titles	425,602
# Periodical titles	1,303
# FTE librarians	10
# Other FTE staff	14
Library annual budget	$1,983,825
Annual circulation	62,591
Annual gate entries	308,146
IC opening date	September 2002
IC name	Information Commons
IC service model type	Primarily integrated services
# Computer workstations	54 in IC, 52 additional workstations for student use in library
What's on desktop	48 PCs and scanners, 6 Macs with large-scale displays
IC architect	Perry, Dean, Rogers (building); Dickinson College staff (IC)
Hours	All hours library is open
IC area	ca. 15,000 sq. ft.
# Physical service points in IC	1
Print reference materials in the IC?	No

Location of Institution and Campus Description

Chartered in 1783 by a most spirited signer of the Declaration of Independence, Dr. Benjamin Rush of Philadelphia, just days after the signing of the Treaty of Paris ended the American Revolution, and named for a signer of the U.S. Constitution, John Dickinson, Dickinson College represents a revolutionary, bold heritage in higher education. The college offers the world—now as then—a distinctively original form of American education and ambition.

Dickinson College offers a four-year program of study in the liberal arts and grants the degrees of bachelor of arts and bachelor of science. The college has 2,255 full-time students, 13 percent of color. Students come from forty states and thirty countries, including 107 international students. Of its 209 faculty, 10 percent are persons of color; 94 percent of the faculty have earned a Ph.D. or other terminal degree. The student-faculty ratio is 11 to 1, and the average class size is eighteen students. Dickinson College is located in Carlisle, Pennsylvania, a center of 20,000 people in the Cumberland Valley of central Pennsylvania.

Information Commons Description

The Dickinson College Information Commons is on the lower level of the Waidner-Spahr Library, a distinctive library building designed by Perry, Dean, Rogers and renovated in 1998. A separate entrance to the library building allows faculty and students to access the Commons from the direction of the student union. The design of the facility departs from similar facilities in its openness and simplicity and reflects an intention to allow its use to evolve as naturally as possible over time. Its materials reflect the motif of the library in its use of maple custom-made furniture.

Information Commons Service Transaction Statistics

Dickinson College does not separate service transactions at the Information Commons since that facility is tightly integrated into the Waidner-Spahr Library. We estimate that users, primarily students, log into Commons workstations 59,268 times per academic year.

Information Commons Staffing and Training

The Information Commons is adjacent to the Department of User Services, a twelve-person department responsible for supporting all desktop systems on campus. The campus help desk is also in that department. In addition, the five-person Academic Technology Services Department maintains office space next to the Commons, facilitating drop-in consultations and service. Finally, a merged library and information technology service desk greets visitors entering the building and provides frontline service to Commons users.

What's on the Desktop

The Information Commons offers forty-eight PCs and scanners and six Macs with large-scale displays. Each PC offers the Microsoft Office suite, and the Macs have equivalent software. All machines are on a three-year replacement cycle.

Information Commons Assessment

The Waidner-Spahr Library has not assessed the Information Commons facility in isolation. The library has in the past administered the LibQUAL+ survey to assess overall use of the library. Its User Services department assesses levels of satisfaction with desktop computing support through a web-based survey distributed to users requesting assistance from the department. Dickinson College also participates with twenty of its peer institutions in the Merged Information Services Organizations survey (the Bryn Mawr Survey). This web-based quantitative survey is designed to measure use and effectiveness for students, faculty, and staff of the services and resources of merged library and computing units.

Information Commons Governance

The Information Commons is managed by the Division of Library and Information Services, a merged library and information technology organization created in 2004. The division is headed by the vice president for library and information services, who reports to the president. The vice president seeks guidance on the development of the Commons from the All College Committee on Information Technology and Services, a governance body consisting of faculty, student, and staff representation.

Lessons Learned

▌ Think of the best location for your Information Commons, then consider not putting it there. When our planning process began, the team assumed that the Commons would be placed at the entrance of the building to achieve high visibility and effect. After using scenario-based planning, the team began to realize that putting it there would cause a traffic jam by concentrating too many essential services in one location. In the end, they decided to build the Commons in the least used part of the library, the lower level of the original 1966 Spahr Library. Paradoxically, this counterintuitive location proved to be very successful, so much so that the library had to open a second entrance to the building in 2004.

▌ In the design of your information commons, consider private sector models such as Barnes and Noble or Starbucks. These companies devote significant resources to understanding how furniture, spacing of furniture, color, and fabrics combine to create memorable spaces. These companies also shape the expectations of students who will be using the Commons.

▌ Consider the design of your information commons to be only your first draft and assume that you will have to reinvest in your facility every year. After all the effort, time, and resources that are spent to develop the commons, it comes as a surprise that the facility is not, in fact, complete. In practice, the creation of the commons only serves to stimulate further demand for technology and services. After its first year of operation, the Dickinson College Information Commons rebuilt its electronic classroom literally from the ground up, added a dozen more workstations, replaced its large-scale monitors, and revamped its service model. The success of the facility drives continuous demand for change.

▌ Build internal critiques into the planning process. The process of designing an information commons can lead to tunnel vision and groupthink as the project team works closely together. Particularly if the planning and consultation process extends over time, the team can become wedded to eccentric or unworkable approaches. In recognition of this risk, the design team at Dickinson College was divided into two subteams: the analysis team and the review team. The analysis subteam consulted with the community, developed alternative scenarios, and prototyped solutions. The review team met with the analysis team and critiqued its work This process prevented the project from "going off the rails" at several junctures.

▌ Take the time to prototype furniture, space use, and technology. Designing an information commons is about working in real time and space. The project team needs to use floor plans and computer tools to explore alternative scenarios, but in the end the facility succeeds only if its actual components work successfully together. In the design of the Dickinson College Information Commons, the project team quickly decided not to use off-the-shelf products but to create its own furniture. It worked with a local cabinetmaker to brainstorm designs. The cabinetmaker created plywood prototypes that could be placed in the Commons space, enabling the project team to move through many design iterations and arrive at optimal solutions.

■ Get used to disruptive, unexpected outcomes. An information commons is not an island in the campus library. It changes how the library is perceived and used. Be prepared for apparently unrelated changes to ripple through the rest of the building. After the success of the Dickinson College Information Commons in the fall of 2002, a staff member likened placing the Commons in a formerly little used part of the building to tipping a canoe. The success of the Commons shifted the balance of the entire library, changing traffic patterns, increasing expectations for information technology, and necessitating the opening of a second entrance to the building. The library staff was challenged to adapt to unexpected and discontinuous change.

■ The convergence of technology and services reflected in the information commons reshapes the role of librarians. They need to "surf" waves of change triggered by the commons can be unnerving for some librarians and exhilarating for others. Without the familiar anchor of the reference desk, librarians find themselves playing new roles and working across organizational boundaries. At Dickinson College, many factors played into the merger of the library and information technology departments in 2004, but the success of the Commons and the model that it presented of integrated services in a space used by students and faculty reflected a need for deep and permanent teamwork that would be embodied by the new Division of Library and Information Services.

ST. PETERSBURG COLLEGE

CARUTH HEALTH EDUCATION CENTER, M. M. BENNETT LIBRARY

Prepared June 2006 by Susan Anderson, Ph.D. (Library Director), Anne Neiberger (Coordinator, New Initiative Program), and Kathy Coughlin (Head Librarian, Health Education Center)

Library website	http://www.spcollege.edu/central/libonline/
Carnegie classification	Associate's–Public 4-Year, Primarily Associate's
# Undergraduates	24,258
# Faculty	1,173
Highest degree offered	Baccalaureate
# Volumes	238,317 collegewide, 10,073 Health Education Center (HEC)
# Titles	222,954 collegewide, 8,473 HEC
# Periodical titles	826
# FTE librarians	13.5 collegewide, 1 HEC
# Other FTE staff	23.5 collegewide, 2.5 HEC
Library annual budget	$2,433,240 collegewide
Annual circulation	88,660 collegewide, 6,020 HEC
Annual gate entries	492,753 collegewide, 65,079 HEC
IC opening date	August 2002
IC name	Health Commons
IC service model type	Integrated services
# Computer workstations	60 PCs, 26 laptops
What's on desktop	Internet, proprietary research databases, Microsoft Office suite, computer-assisted instructional modules, medical dictionaries, dosage calculator program, ANGEL (course delivery system), board reviews, student test banks, frequently used informational sites, interactive physiology software
IC architect	Susan Reiter/Vivian DeRussy, in-house design
Hours	Mon.–Thurs. 7:30 a.m.–9:00 p.m.; Fri. 7:30 a.m.–4:00 p.m.; Sat. 10:00 a.m.–5:00 p.m.
IC area	14,021 sq. ft.
# Physical service points in IC	7
Average # IC users in a typical month	7,308 (82/215 users/11.25 months/year)
Print reference materials in the IC?	Yes, 1,338

Location of Institution and Campus Description

The Health Education Center of St. Petersburg College, St. Petersburg, Florida, houses the allied health and nursing programs. The Center is centrally located in the geographic area that St. Petersburg College serves, providing easy access to students within the entire service area. There are eleven associate degree programs and four baccalaureate programs: dental hygiene, emergency medical services, funeral services, health information management, human services, medical laboratory technology, nursing, physical therapist assistant, radiography, respiratory care, and veterinary technology. One graduate program is offered at the Health Education Center, delivered through a partnership with a university in order to further meet the workforce needs of the community.

The Health Education Center's programs educate students with state-of-the-art equipment, including human patient simulators. To increase student success in these programs, the Center provides a wide range of tutoring services from improving math skills to teaching the complexities of disease pathology. One intent of maximizing student success is to expand the workforce for the health care industry.

Information Commons Description

Old-fashioned straight tables and chairs were removed, and the library was furnished with connecting computer stations that allow for more than one student to work at a computer. Areas were allocated for quiet work and noisy study. Students thrived in this new space. It was a dramatic change from the quiet and traditional library space of the past.

In 2005, more than 2,000 square feet of space adjacent to the library was remodeled to house the New Initiative Program tutorial lab and offices. One door opens into the library, and staff are negotiating for another, more inviting opening between the tutorial lab and the library to create a more

natural flow of staff and students between the two areas. This new area will include a student lounge with refrigerator and tables to give busy students a nearby break area.

Information Commons Service Transaction Statistics

We recorded 1,701 transactions per month, suggesting 19,142 per year on the basis of an 11.25-month year.

Information Commons Staffing and Training

All new hires attend a college-sponsored orientation. Tutors are familiarized on a needs basis in their areas of expertise. Adjunct librarians attend training sessions designed for all college adjunct faculty. Emphasis is placed on health-related backgrounds in hiring librarians and adjunct librarians. In addition to specific training, tutors, librarians, and adjunct librarians are strongly encouraged to attend the numerous staff development opportunities provided by the college.

Professional staffing for the Health Commons is provided continuously during the 70 weekly operational hours. The tutoring area is staffed by a minimum of one professional tutor. Tutoring services are augmented with subject-specific expertise tutoring on an as-needed basis. The reference desk is manned during all operating hours.

What's on the Desktop

Available on the Health Commons computers are the Internet, proprietary research databases, the Microsoft Office suite, computer-assisted instructional modules, two medical dictionaries, a dosage calculator program, ANGEL (course delivery system), board reviews, student test banks, frequently used informational sites, and interactive physiology software.

Information Commons Assessment

St. Petersburg College annually conducts a satisfaction survey of enrolled students. The survey has specific questions regarding library and tutorial services. The library has for the past ten years conducted an annual library survey and for the past two years a faculty survey. The Learning Support Centers are now conducting annual surveys of students. In 2005 a common survey for all campuses was developed. Statistics are recorded for gate count (entry), circulation, reference questions, computer assistance, and tutorial questions.

Information Commons Governance

The executive vice president of the college oversees both the campuses and the college libraries. The Health Education campus has a campus provost reporting to the executive vice president. New Initiative Program, the information commons, reports to the campus provost. The campus library reports to the director of libraries, who reports to the executive vice president. The libraries and the campus Learning Support Centers form an oversight group chaired by the director of libraries. The oversight group sets goals and measurable objectives and presents an annual report of progress to the executive vice president and the College Cabinet. The oversight group meets regularly. The coordinator of information commons is the cochair of the learning support services subcommittee of the oversight group. Collaboration and cooperation are the tools that make this system of governance viable.

Lessons Learned

▌ Combining library and tutorial services has greatly increased the use of library and tutorial services. The most important factor in success is the willingness of staff to collaborate, experiment, and cooperate. With cooperation and administrative support, all things are possible. Whenever we were (or still are) having needs along the way, either our director of libraries, provost, or associate provost came through with innovative ideas plus the dollars to help. The Health Commons continues to evolve, with plans for a new connecting door and a student snack lounge.

▌ The Health Commons has become a vehicle to share resources and to provide seamless access to those combined resources for students, but, of equal importance, this information commons has created a community. Historically, the atmosphere of the library was welcoming, but there was a feeling of impersonality among the students. The atmosphere of the tutoring center has always been more intimate and warm. Since the establishment of the information commons, there has been a more caring and communicative atmosphere in both the library and the tutoring center areas of the commons. Some students were uncomfortable with the idea of talking being allowed in the "quiet" library. With our insightful design including a "quiet room," these students learned the benefit of being allowed to study in groups and then retreat to the quiet area when necessary. This was all facilitated by positive staff who had bought into the idea. An environment in which students feel accepted and nurtured, and in which they feel part of the whole, leads to a lessening of anxiety and isolation. This, in turn, surely must contribute to student success.

▌ Change is an ongoing process that is sometimes painful for both students and staff. The administrators need to remember to keep the communication lines open and really listen to expressions of concern.

chapter eight

Lessons Learned

Frequently the best advice comes from frontline practitioners who have tested the waters and are willing to share their "lessons learned" with commons colleagues. Each of the institutions included in the information commons case studies presented in chapters 6 and 7 was asked the following questions:

> What are the most important "lessons learned" from your particular information commons?

> As you look ahead (perhaps ten years down the road), please suggest ideas about what would be most important to your library if you were to re-create or renovate your information commons.

> If you could begin from scratch right now, what things would you do differently for more effective, long-term results?

Below we present a sample of edited excerpts from the responses of these twenty information commons.

Assessment

Abilene Christian University

■ We would try to insert, at strategic points in the planning process, a fuller discussion of assessment issues. A more systematic, continuing analysis would ensure that we are asking the most appropriate questions at the right time.

Asbury Theological Seminary

▌ We know from observation that the use of our facility has increased significantly since the implementation of our information commons. It would have been better to have statistics rather than anecdotal information.

▌ The information commons environment is dynamic and always changing. We cannot afford to become complacent or feel like we have "arrived."

▌ Watch and learn from what others are doing in other information commons.

Design

Dickinson College

▌ In the design of your information commons, consider private sector models such as Barnes and Noble and Starbucks. Private companies devote significant resources to understanding how furniture, color, and fabrics combine to create memorable spaces. These companies shape the expectations of students who will be using the information commons.

▌ Consider the design of your information commons to be only your first draft and assume that you will have to reinvest in your facility every year.

University of Georgia

▌ Move to create programmatic spaces for more tutoring opportunities and academic-oriented programs and less space as meeting spaces for nonacademic student events. This might also involve the creation of private collaboration labs for group projects.

▌ It is imperative that all those involved with the administration of the space and programs embrace flexibility in their assumptions of how the space should be used, in policymaking, even in assumptions about "what a library is," down to the smallest details such as what color markers to

provide for the whiteboards in the group study rooms, service desk location, vending machine placement, or provision of staplers. Be prepared to change policies (sometimes many times), be open to how the students and faculty want and need to use the space, and revamp accordingly.

▌ Create flexible spaces that are open and can be used in different ways. The more flexible the space, the easier and less expensive it will be to make changes.

Equipment

Indiana University Bloomington

▌ If the libraries were to renovate or re-create the information commons, they would incorporate more power outlets for public use into the design and they would get more durable, darker furniture and carpet.

University of Massachusetts Amherst

▌ More PCs

▌ More loaner tablet PCs

▌ A technological solution to show open stations and rooms, announcements, event information, and system outage notices

▌ Heavy-duty printers to handle large PDFs efficiently

▌ Color printers

▌ More tables with convenient power to use laptops and wireless

▌ Sound-absorbing features

Funding

University of Arizona

▌ The furniture and carpet have taken a real pounding. Make sure to include a furniture refresh budget in your planning.

Dickinson College

❚ We underestimated how the initial success of the information commons would create a level of demand that outstripped our resources. We might have worked with the college to create a financial reserve to respond more rapidly to increased user demand.

❚ Secure more dedicated funding for implementation, particularly to address furniture issues and building additional collaborative spaces.

Governance

University of Georgia

❚ Be well prepared to address the problems inherent in managing the operation of a building of this size and scope, especially with regard to staffing, technical problems, and security systems.

University of Guelph

❚ Develop a clear governance structure and budgeting process from the outset.

Location

California Polytechnic State University

❚ The location of a commons is vitally important in shaping how it is perceived and how it is used over time.

❚ In retrospect, if it were possible to locate the learning commons at the very front of the building, within easy view of the entrance, then it would be immediately visible to much of the campus. This would increase curiosity about the purpose of the commons in the university and increase visits to the commons itself. A prominent location would also allow the commons to promote the work it creates more easily by rotating wall-sized projections of the work being accomplished inside.

Brigham Young University

❚ The space chosen for the commons is the best space in the library. It is constantly used throughout the year during any time the library is open.

Partners

Binghamton University

❚ Our biggest lesson has been the challenge of blending the services and resources of two campus units with very different cultures: the Libraries and Computing Services and Educational Technology. Each unit has a unique mission orientation and focus. Using the services of an objective facilitator was extremely helpful in the collaboration process. Also, the joint service standards we established for the commons helped us keep our focus and work together toward the common goal of establishing a high-quality service, research, and computing environment.

❚ The inclusion of additional student support services (e.g., paper-writing assistance or tutoring) within or nearby the commons would be a real benefit to students, even as small satellite stations with limited hours.

St. Petersburg College

❚ Collaboration between the tutoring center and library has resulted in staff developing and implementing innovative ideas that would never have arisen had the two entities remained isolated. There is tremendous enthusiasm among the staff, and that enthusiasm appears to have been adopted by the students.

❚ Our commons has provided a vehicle to share resources and to provide seamless access to those combined resources for students, but, of equal importance, the information commons has created a community. Historically, the atmosphere of the library was welcoming, but there was a feeling of impersonality among the students. The atmosphere of the tutoring center has always been more intimate and warm. Since the establishment of the information commons, there has been a more caring and communicative atmosphere in both the library and the tutoring center areas of the commons. The actual physical moving of the tutoring center to a joint area with the library was the most important space idea. Students now think of the commons as a combined team.

Policies

University of Victoria

▌ Create a timely way to make decisions regarding requests for peripherals, additional software, and the like.

▌ Create a plan for queuing.

▌ Have a process in place to respond to requests for additional software and peripherals—we have spent far too much time figuring this out piecemeal.

Public Relations/Promotion

California Polytechnic State University

▌ In the next ten years, we would like to move much of the public face for the learning commons directly into the center of campus life by promoting the work of the commons on screens and walls all over campus.

▌ Good and seemingly obvious ideas, centers, and organizations always need basic and devoted promotion to ensure they become visible in the public mind and to demonstrate their essential benefits continually to the world surrounding them. If you build it, they don't always come.

▌ We could have identified faculty or student advocates to shape the public vision of the learning commons so that better orchestrated

promotion of the commons would have occurred all across campus.

▌ A series of public activities with a high-attention factor (musical performances, theater presentations, film events) could have taken place in the middle of the commons during its first few weeks of being open to the public.

▌ The initiative for the creation of the learning commons really needed to be driven ahead by the deans of all the Cal Poly colleges working together. This top-level agreement would have strengthened the financial and academic standing of the commons from the beginning.

▌ Creating a new gallery/lobby area for the commons to provide an easy walk-through space might more effectively promote the projects connected with the commons.

Services

University of Southern California

▌ Add support for web-based videoconferencing.

▌ Experiment with supporting mobile technologies: circulating podcasting kits, videoconferencing kits, and collaboration kits.

▌ Collaborative workroom reservation: Because of high demand, students often abuse the reservation process: reservation logs disappear, reservations are crossed out, reservation policy is ignored, and so forth. This issue requires desk staff to mediate reservation disputes and settle arguments on the reservation policy. Currently, the staff are collaborating with information technology consultants to review room reservation software to implement an online reservation system.

Space

Abilene Christian University

▌ We were aware from the beginning that construction of the learning commons would create reevaluation, displacement, and movement of existing collections, departments, service points, and staff. We thought carefully about departments that would be permanently displaced but, given another opportunity, we would budget more generously for temporary locations of other library units and activities.

University of Arizona

▌ We did a great job at creating a collaborative computing space. Our challenge now is to create other areas in the libraries for quiet computing.

▌ We were forced to add some new construction to currently existing space, with the result that the configuration of the room is not conducive to funneling users with questions to the reference desk. We think we would get more people asking us questions if the help desk was more of a focal point, but the layout of the existing building prevents this.

Staff

Carleton College

▌ Recognize that it is difficult for many people to visualize a new layout, leading them to reject changes initially. It is vital that you not only find ways to help staff and other campus constituencies understand why there are changes but also provide multiple ways to visualize those changes.

University of Georgia

▌ The reference librarians role has changed to a role more in line with the tasks of teaching, digital design, and public relations. Students and faculty do not always make the connection that this space is a library. This affects how they use the reference services, particularly the reference librarians for help with research.

▌ The overall theory of integrated "one-stop shopping" will continue to be successful. After continued assessment of the use of the reference librarians at the desk, reevaluation of the level of library staffing

at the desk should be made so that more energy can be put forward into liaison with faculty in the classroom and the building of other programs.

Theory/Concept

California Polytechnic State University

▌ Even noble, supportive, and truly beneficial ideas are never exempt from considerations of politics and institutional turf disputes. Politics are always local.

Indiana University Bloomington

▌ The information commons is one part of a much larger picture, and its future will grow within that context. The type of renovation or any changes to the commons will depend on the types of services and space available for faculty, graduate students, and undergraduate students. Ideally we would develop academic and technologically rich environments for all users and design them around their research and information needs.

Users

University of Arizona

▌ Information commons users won't necessarily be traditional library users. They won't necessarily ask great numbers of questions.

Carleton College

▌ Be very tuned in to what is new or even breaking in the student's world so that the library is not reacting to social forces but ready to meet the students where they are.

Conclusions from Lessons Learned

Common threads that permeate the above, more detailed "lessons learned" include these:

ASSESSMENT

▌ Begin your information commons with an evaluation program in place.

- Collect hard data (rather than anecdotal information) to support making changes or asking for additional funding.
- Listen carefully to suggestions and complaints from students.

DESIGN

- Design flexibility into commons spaces (moveable walls or no walls, modular furnishings).
- Provide for varied learning environments (collaborative/social spaces, quiet spaces).
- Include sound-absorbing features.
- Emulate private sector design models such as at Barnes and Noble or Starbucks.
- Allow for plenty of high-speed wireless access points.
- Don't allow sightlines to be obscured by columns, high furnishings, or other obstacles.
- Make obvious the locations of important facilities (classrooms, elevators).
- Plan service desks carefully with regard to size, location, and modularity.

EQUIPMENT

- Select modular furnishings (everything interlocking or on wheels for easy regrouping).
- Select furnishings to support wireless computing (where students can use laptops and keep them powered).
- Select furnishings with low sides so that it is apparent when a workstation is available.
- Provide plenty of loaner laptops.
- Provide plenty of multimedia creation stations.
- Provide heavy-duty printers to handle large PDFs efficiently.

FUNDING

- Secure dedicated funding for implementation.
- Include a technology and furniture/carpeting "refresh budget" in your planning.

GOVERNANCE

- Develop a clear governance structure from the start.
- Consider developing a memorandum of understanding when taking on partners.

LOCATION

- Place the information commons at the front or entrance of a facility.
- Make your information commons highly visible for the best chances for success.

PARTNERS

- Proactively recruit collaborative partners (such as IT, Writing Center, Tutoring Center, Faculty Center for Teaching Excellence, coffeeshop) to ensure the success of your information commons.

POLICIES

- Develop clearly articulated policies from the start.

PUBLIC RELATIONS

- Offer a series of high-attention public activities within your information commons.
- Make use of social networking resources (MySpace, Facebook, wikis, RSS feeds) to publicize your information commons.

SERVICES

- Situate one-stop-shopping points (integrated services) for user convenience.

- Provide a communication mechanism between workstations and staff so a user does not have to leave his workstation to get assistance.

SPACE

- Think carefully about the size and location of the print reference collection.

- Create group study rooms in a variety of sizes.

- Create simple group work spaces (with collaborative furnishings and workstations) out on the floor of the commons. This requires less space and expense than separate group study rooms.

STAFF

- Make sure you have staff working in the information commons who value the customer and know how to deliver good service.

- Get more staff buy-in through more and better staff training and participation.

- Recognize that the reference librarian's role is changing to reflect the needs of the information commons.

THEORY/CONCEPT

- Recognize that the information commons is a building block for information literacy.

- Recognize that the information commons changes how the library is perceived and used.

- Understand that to produce the best service model you need to focus on user needs.

USERS

- Be very tuned in to what is new or breaking in the students' world so that the information commons can meet the students where they are.

appendix A

Sample Brand and Graphics

PROVIDENCE
COLLEGE

the **Library + Commons**
Patron- centered design & focus

Support Station
Second Floor

Staffed daily by research
support staff

Access to scanners

INFORMATION STATION

CREATION STATION

What Is The *Library + Commons@Phillips Memorial Library*?

The *Library + Commons* is the seamless integration of the
Traditional Library ↔ with the ↔ Technology-Rich Commons.

The Traditional Library
-- books, face-to-face services and interactions, etc. --
↔ + ↔
The Technology-Rich Commons
-- electronic resources, anytime-anywhere services and interactions --

The *Library + Commons* is the library *designed & focused exclusively on patron needs*:
- Point of Need: <u>where</u> patrons are in their work:
  reflection→ research→analysis→synthesis→processing-to-product→evaluation
- Level of Need: freshmen, graduate, faculty research
- Time of Need: anytime, 24/7
- Place of Need: in-library, dorm, across town, the country, the world: anywhere
- Format of Need: although we often guide patrons to the entire collected series, the book, chapter, or journal article, our patrons prefer, and are accustomed to, using key-word searches (Google, etc.) to find *only* the page, the chart, graph, sentence or phrase
- Speed of Need: although we often prefer that patrons spend **10-45 minutes** *with us* to find the best collection of information for their research needs, they often prefer to do quicker searching and fill their need in less than **5 minutes**, often in **30 seconds** or less

The *Library + Commons* offers the patron <u>the continuum of services and resources</u>:
- Comfortable, aesthetically-pleasing surroundings: chairs, sofas, lounges, collaborative spaces, art, cared-for areas: the *library as place*
- Friendly, helpful, capable staff: desired *affect of service* at desks, pleasant, helpful, "roving" staff, staff who are there when the patrons needs assistance
  - **Information Station:** main floor, staffed 8 am-11:00 pm/midnight most days by research support staff, with two collaborative PC stations and one collaborative Macintosh station with double monitors, shareable wireless keyboards and mice, a scanner, variable furniture for use in flexible ways for collaboration
  - **Support Station:** second floor, staffed many hours each day by research support staff with access to scanners
  - **Creation Station/Macintosh Lab:** main floor, accessible during all library hours, supported by *Library + Commons* staff at all times with computers and scanners
  - **Digital Services Lab:** main floor, staffed 10 am–10 pm most days by expert digitization support staff with access to PC and Macintosh computers and scanners
- Easily accessible information resources in all formats – paper (in-house, HELIN loan, interlibrary loan), electronic, microform – all *in* or *from within* the library or *from wherever the patron is* – *informational control*

PROVIDENCE
COLLEGE

- Richesse of technology in the _Library + Commons_
  - 50 high-end desktop PCs with DVD/RW capabilities, and MSOffice+; 4 PCs also have scanners
  - 18 high-end desktop PCs with DVD/RW capabilities and MSOffice+ in the electronic classroom
  - 29 laptops for student check-out with MSOffice+
  - 5 high-end iMac Macintosh computers and scanners with Microsoft Office, Adobe Creative Suite, and Apple iLife software
  - Digital Services Lab with 2 high-end PCs and 2 Macintosh computers, scanners for various formats, and full range of productivity & digitization software
  - Wireless 802.11 a, b, and g access for College and patron computers
  - 10 high-end scanners (8½"x11" and 11"x17") with Photoshop image manipulation and OCR/Optical Character Recognition software
  - 6 public printers (color printing options in the future)
  - 5 public scanners on the main floor, 2 public scanners on the second floor, and additional format scanners in the Digital Services Lab
- Spaces for collaboration
  - 3 open group study rooms with high-end PCs for 8 to 9 persons
  - 1 open group study/presentation rehearsal room for up to 25 persons with data projector and screen, available laptop computer and video recorder
  - Macintosh Creation Station with high-end iMacs and scanner
  - Wireless laptops available for checkout to enhance technology tools
  - Information Station desk with 3 collaboration stations each with computer, double-monitor, wireless keyboard and mouse, and ample comfortable & versatile furniture
- Access to tools: high-technology, electric/manual small & large staplers, small & large hole-punches, pencils/pens, paper-clips, etc.
- Access to refreshments: gourmet hot drinks on ground floor, drinks in covered containers allowed in the building

Into the Future:

The _Library + Commons_ will perhaps:

- Add more Macintosh computers, scanners and laptops for checkout, and more collaborative group study spaces over time, as patron use and preferences suggest;
- Provide more refreshments over time, as patron use and preferences suggest; and
- Provide extended hours over time, as patron use and preferences suggest.

Still the central components of the _Library + Commons_ will remain the same:

- _Explicitly focused on patron needs_
- _Seamless integration of the traditional high-touch Library with high-tech Commons_
- _The full range of resources enabling and facilitating all academic research activities from reflection→ research→analysis→synthesis→processing-to-product→evaluation_

PROVIDENCE
COLLEGE

appendix B

Sample Information Commons Survey

Library Survey Sent to Faculty and Students, University of North Carolina at Charlotte

The J. Murrey Atkins Library at the University of North Carolina at Charlotte created and used this web-based survey in spring 2007 using the proprietary electronic resource Surveyshare. UNCC received more than 1,400 responses in one week by sending a "request for participation e-mail" with a link to this survey to all UNCC faculty and students. Surveyshare maintained a running tabulation of all survey responses that included not only number and percentage counts but also visual interpretation of responses via graphs and pie charts. This survey might serve as an adaptable model for other libraries.

UNCC Atkins Library Survey

1. **How often do you come into the library building?**
   - ❏ Daily
   - ❏ Several times a week
   - ❏ Several times a month
   - ❏ Several times a semester
   - ❏ Once a semester
   - ❏ First time user
   - ❏ Never

2. **If you have never come into the library, may we ask why?**

3. Have you ever asked for assistance (in person, by telephone or e-mail) from one of the library's public service desks?

    ❏ Yes

    ❏ No

4. Were staff at the service desk helpful and friendly?

    ❏ Extremely satisfied

    ❏ Very satisfied

    ❏ Somewhat satisfied

    ❏ Not very satisfied

    ❏ Not applicable

5. Were staff at the service desk able to answer your questions?

    ❏ Extremely satisfied

    ❏ Very satisfied

    ❏ Somewhat satisfied

    ❏ Not very satisfied

    ❏ Not applicable

6. Were you assisted by the Circulation Desk (checking out, renewing and returning books, laptops, AV equipment)?

    ❏ Yes

    ❏ No

7. How satisfied were you with the Circulation Desk's assistance?

    ❏ Extremely satisfied

    ❏ Very satisfied

    ❏ Somewhat satisfied

    ❏ Not very satisfied

    ❏ Not applicable

8. Were you assisted by the Information Desk (Group Study Rooms, referrals to other service desks and staff)?

    ❏ Yes

    ❏ No

9. How satisfied were you with the Information Desk's assistance?

   ❑ Extremely satisfied

   ❑ Very satisfied

   ❑ Somewhat satisfied

   ❑ Not very satisfied

   ❑ Not applicable

10. Were you assisted by the Presentation Support Desk (assistance with productivity software, wireless, scanning and multimedia labs, etc.)?

   ❑ Yes

   ❑ No

11. How satisfied were you with the Presentation Support Desk's assistance?

   ❑ Extremely satisfied

   ❑ Very satisfied

   ❑ Somewhat satisfied

   ❑ Not very satisfied

   ❑ Not at all satisfied

   ❑ Not applicable

12. Were you assisted by the Reference Desk (research assistance, electronic searching, etc.)?

   ❑ Yes

   ❑ No

13. How satisfied were you with the Reference Desk's assistance?

   ❑ Extremely satisfied

   ❑ Very satisfied

   ❑ Somewhat satisfied

   ❑ Not very satisfied

   ❑ Not applicable

14. Were you assisted by the Collections Desk on the second floor (reserve materials, periodicals, etc.)?

   ❑ Yes

   ❑ No

15. How satisfied were you with the Collection Desk's assistance?

☐ Extremely satisfied

☐ Very satisfied

☐ Somewhat satisfied

☐ Not very satisfied

☐ Not applicable

16. Do you have any comments (likes/dislikes; praise/suggestions) about any of the public service desks mentioned above?

17. Are you satisfied that the library helps you meet your learning/research needs?

☐ Extremely satisfied

☐ Very satisfied

☐ Somewhat satisfied

☐ Not very satisfied

☐ Not at all satisfied

18. What should the library do differently to help you meet your learning/research needs?

19. What difficulties/barriers (if any) have you encountered while using the library?

20. How often do you use Atkins Library resources from outside of the building?

☐ Daily

☐ Several times a week

☐ Several times a month

☐ Several times a semester

☐ Once a semester

☐ First time user

☐ Never

21. Do you find the library welcoming?

☐ Extremely welcoming

☐ Very welcoming

☐ Somewhat welcoming

☐ Not very welcoming

☐ Not at all welcoming

☐ Never been in the library

22. Do you find the library safe?

- ❏ Extremely safe
- ❏ Very safe
- ❏ Somewhat safe
- ❏ Not very safe
- ❏ Not at all safe
- ❏ Never been in the library

23. Do you find the library clean?

- ❏ Extremely clean
- ❏ Very clean
- ❏ Somewhat clean
- ❏ Not very clean
- ❏ Not at all clean
- ❏ Never been in the library

24. Do you have any further comments about the library's physical appearance?

25. What do you do in the library? (Mark all that apply)

- ❏ Consult librarians and other staff; get research assistance
- ❏ Use software
- ❏ Get technical assistance
- ❏ Participate in class-related activities
- ❏ Participate in personal/recreational computer usage
- ❏ Study with a group or another student
- ❏ Use computer between classes
- ❏ Check out books and/or equipment or laptops
- ❏ Never been in the library
- ❏ Other:

26. Which of the following tools and services do you usually use while in the library? (Mark all that apply)

- ❏ Reference/Research Service
- ❏ PC Workstation
- ❏ Assistive Tech. Equipment (for users with disabilities)
- ❏ Group Study Rooms
- ❏ Mac Workstation
- ❏ Photocopy Machines
- ❏ Print Stations
- ❏ Handouts and Brochures
- ❏ Technical Assistance
- ❏ Never been in the library
- ❏ Other:

27. **How satisfied are you with the library's public computers?**

❒ Extremely satisfied

❒ Very satisfied

❒ Somewhat satisfied

❒ Not very satisfied

❒ Not at all satisfied

❒ Not applicable

28. **Have you ever had to wait for a computer?**

❒ Yes

❒ No

❒ Not applicable

29. **If you've had to wait for a computer, how long has your wait been?**

❒ 10 min. or less

❒ 10–20 min.

❒ 20–30 min.

❒ 30–45 min.

❒ Over 45 min.

❒ Not applicable

30. **Do you have any comments about the library's public computers?**

31. **How satisfied are you with the library's multimedia and scanning services?**

❒ Extremely satisfied

❒ Very satisfied

❒ Somewhat satisfied

❒ Not very satisfied

❒ Not at all satisfied

❒ Not applicable

32. **How satisfied are you with the library's group study room facilities?**

❒ Extremely satisfied

❒ Very satisfied

❒ Somewhat satisfied

❒ Not very satisfied

❒ Not at all satisfied

❒ Not applicable

33. What do you like MOST about the library?

34. What would you like to change or improve about the library?

35. When you are in the library, do you usually work
- ❏ Alone
- ❏ As part of a group
- ❏ Alone AND as part of a group
- ❏ Not applicable

36. What days do you visit the library?
- ❏ Sunday
- ❏ Monday
- ❏ Tuesday
- ❏ Wednesday
- ❏ Thursday
- ❏ Friday
- ❏ Saturday
- ❏ Not applicable

37. What time of the day do you visit the library?
- ❏ Morning
- ❏ Early afternoon
- ❏ Late afternoon
- ❏ Early evening (6–9 p.m.)
- ❏ Late evening (9 p.m.–midnight)
- ❏ Not applicable

38. How much time do you usually spend in the library per visit?
- ❏ Less than an hour
- ❏ 1–3 hours
- ❏ 3–5 hours
- ❏ More than 5 hours
- ❏ Not applicable
- ❏ Other:

39. Are you satisfied with the current arrangement of public service desks, computers, study areas, and collections on the library's first floor?

❑ Yes

❑ No

40. Presently there are four service desks on the first floor of the library: Circulation, Information, Presentation Support, and Reference. If you could rearrange the desks, would you

❑ Leave things the way they are; no changes

❑ Keep the number of desks the same but relocate them throughout the first floor

❑ Merge the existing four desks into three desks (eliminate one existing desk and reassign its current services to other desks)

❑ Merge the existing four desks into two desks (eliminate two existing desks and reassign their services to other desks)

❑ Eliminate three service desks and combine all services at one desk

❑ No opinion

❑ Other:

41. If you were to redesign the arrangement of public computers on the library's first floor, would you

❑ Leave things the way they are; no changes

❑ Add more work space around each computer

❑ Add more stand-up workstations for quick checks of e-mail

❑ Add more tables with electrical outlets near the wireless hot spots

❑ No opinion

❑ Other:

42. Of the following suggested changes for the library's first floor, please RANK 1-2-3 your top 3 choices with 1 being most important, 3 least important.

	1	2	3
More group workspaces within the open areas of the 1st floor	❑	❑	❑
More group workspaces within enclosed Group Study Rooms	❑	❑	❑
More individual computer workstations	❑	❑	❑
More comfortable upholstered chairs, sofas, etc.	❑	❑	❑
More quiet no-click individual study spaces	❑	❑	❑
Movable furnishing areas	❑	❑	❑
More social spaces	❑	❑	❑
More print stations	❑	❑	❑

	1	2	3
More photocopy machines	❏	❏	❏
Designated space for cell phone use	❏	❏	❏
Other	❏	❏	❏
None	❏	❏	❏

43. **If you were to locate additional student services in the library, what would you prefer? Please RANK 1-2-3 your top 3 choices with 1 being most important, 3 least important.**

	1	2	3
Include writing assistance	❏	❏	❏
Include tutoring assistance	❏	❏	❏
Include a 24/7 work area	❏	❏	❏
Include a media room (with TV news programs, etc.)	❏	❏	❏
Include public programs (art exhibits, lecture series, etc.)	❏	❏	❏
Other	❏	❏	❏
None	❏	❏	❏

44. **In considering new library services, how important do you consider the following? Please RANK 1-2-3 your top 3 choices with 1 being most important, 3 least important.**

	1	2	3
Self-booking of Group Study Rooms	❏	❏	❏
More self check-out of library materials	❏	❏	❏
Other	❏	❏	❏

45. **Do you have any suggestions for other library services?**

Glossary

Collaborative learning. Learners in small groups working together on the same task simultaneously to develop their own answers through interaction and consensus.

Collaborative space. An area within the commons, such as a group study room or classroom, that is configured for two or more persons to work together.

Commons. Sets of resources (both cultural and natural) that a community recognizes as being accessible to any member of that community.

Computer consultants (see also Navigation assistants). Assistants who are trained to assist with software and hardware in the information commons.

Creative commons. The broad social and cultural arena of free speech, shared knowledge, and human expression in the Digital Age that encompasses ideas such as fair use and public domain.

Digital commons. An electronic pool of knowledge accessed via the Web.

Discrete service points. Several different service points within an information commons, each offering a different kind of services (e.g., separate desks for reference assistance and multimedia support services); the opposite of integrated services or "one-stop shopping."

Electronic classroom. A collaborative area that offers instruction to students within a computer lab setting.

Faculty center for teaching. A faculty support or development center that provides assistance and resources in the areas of pedagogy and instructional technology.

Information commons. A model for information service delivery that offers patrons integrated access to (and expert assistance with) electronic information resources, multimedia, productivity software, print resources, and services.

Information commons desk. The first point of public service contact within the information commons, providing basic directional and informational assistance, referrals, machine operation assistance, and troubleshooting.

Information Commons Discussion Group, Association of College and Research Libraries, American Library Association. This discussion group was approved by ACRL in June 2005 and is open to all who wish to share knowledge about information/learning commons.

Integrated service point. A "one-stop" services point (usually staffed by both reference librarians and information technologists) that provides assistance in the identification, location, retrieval, and manipulation of information.

Learning commons. The transformation of information commons to learning commons reflects a shift in learning theory from transmission of knowledge to creation of knowledge and self-direction in learning. A learning commons includes all aspects of the information commons, but to a greater extent. The learning commons is not library-centric but, instead, strategically aligned with the institution-wide vision and mission as an active partner in the broad educational enterprise.

Multimedia station. Information commons multimedia stations (high-end personal computers) provide tools to help students with projects involving web design and digital audio and video manipulation.

Navigation assistants. Student assistants who move about the commons floor helping patrons with hardware and software questions.

Physical commons. Sections, floors, or departments within libraries (or facilities apart from libraries) designed to organize workspace, technology, and service delivery around the integrated digital environment.

Research commons. A physical facility primarily for faculty and graduate students that complements the information commons. Here faculty and graduate students can consult with library and IT staff to learn how to use, create, manipulate, and preserve research data. This facility also provides assistance with grant and compliance issues, copyright and intellectual property policy, and assistance for researchers in technology transfer.

Strategic planning. Long-range planning covering a period of three to five years that includes setting goals, strategies, and objectives for programs. Strategic plans usually include (1) a diagnosis of the organization's external and internal environments, (2) vision and mission statements, (3) overall goals, (4) strategies to be pursued, and (5) allocation of resources to achieve the organization's goals.

Tactical planning. Short-range planning that usually has a one- to two-year time span, deals primarily with the implementation phase of the planning process, and is tightly integrated with the annual budget process.

Tompkins, Philip. Philip Tompkins, the director of library information services at Maricopa Community College's Estrella Mountain Community Center, Arizona, in the early 1990s, is often credited with developing the information commons service model, which evolved from his planning for new learning environments within the Maricopa County Community College District—specifically his plans for the renovation of the existing library at Mesa Community College and his design of the new campus at Estrella Mountain Community College.

Tragedy of the commons. Metaphor used to illustrate the conflict between individual interests and the common good. Within a common pool of resources, overuse or unfair use of these resources creates problems, often destroying its sustainability.

Bibliography

Websites

Coalition for Networked Information, Collaborative Facilities. http://www
.dartmouth.edu/~collab/.

Dartmouth College and Coalition for Networked Information.

Henning, Joanne. "Information Commons Study Leave." http://jhenning.law.uvic.ca.

Personal website of Joanne Henning, Head, Reference Services,
McPherson Library, University of Victoria, British Columbia. Notes and
images from her IC site visits.

Herman Miller Online White Papers. http://www.hermanmiller.com/CDA/
SSA/WhitePapers/0,1599,a10-c77-k25,00.html.

Papers include "A View of the Changing Campus: How Learning
Environments Can Support Changes in Higher Education"; "Creating
a Culture of Sustainability: How Campuses Are Taking the Lead"; and
"Paradigm Shift: How Higher Education Is Improving Learning."

IC Flickr . . . Infocommons. http://www.flickr.com/search/?q=infocommons.

Inspiring variety of site photos posted by information commons from all
types of institutions.

INFOCOMMONS-L@LISTSERV.BINGHAMTON.EDU. http://www
.lsoft.com/scripts/wl.exe?SL1=INFOCOMMONS-L&H=LISTSERV
.BINGHAMTON.EDU.

This listserv, hosted by SUNY Binghamton, maintains an extremely
helpful archive of advice on such IC topics as assessment, budget, flexible
floor plans, food/beverage policies, furniture, laptop requirements,
mission and vision statements, noise control, print reference collections,
printing issues, restricting computer use, roving student assistants,
vending machines, and writing/tutoring centers.

The listserv was inaugurated by Dave Vose (Head of Reference and
Electronic Services, Bartle Library, Binghamton University, Binghamton,
N.Y.) in May 2004. The majority of listserv members represent libraries at

higher education institutions in the United States and Canada, with public libraries and special libraries also represented. A July 2006 snapshot showed a total of 640 listserv subscribers from information commons around the world, including Australia, Canada, Germany, Hong Kong, and South Africa as well as the United States.

J. Murrey Atkins Library (UNCC) Information Commons website. http://library.uncc.edu/infocommons/.

Includes speakers' documents from several information commons programs sponsored by ACRL 2003–2007:

"Information Commons Issues and Trends: Voices from the Front-Line—Colorado State University, Emory University, University of Arizona, University of NC Charlotte, University of Southern California, Elon University (NC), Brookdale Community College (NJ)." Association of College and Research Libraries National Conference 2003, Charlotte, N.C.

"Information Commons 101: Nuts and Bolts Planning." Association of College and Research Libraries Pre-Conference, Jan. 9, 2004, San Diego, Calif.

"Information Commons 101: Nuts and Bolts Planning." Association of College and Research Libraries Pre-Conference, June 25, 2004, Orlando, Fla.

"From Information Commons to Learning Commons." Association of College and Research Libraries National Conference 2005, Minneapolis, Minn.

"Information Commons: Staffing Models and Staff Training—Panel Program." ALA Midwinter Conference 2006, Information Commons Discussion Group, San Antonio, Tex.

"The Commons—Libraries as Dynamic Learning Spaces." ALA Annual Conference 2006. Information Commons Discussion Group, New Orleans, La.

"Exploring and Forging Collaborative Relationships between an Information Commons and Others on Campus." ALA Annual Conference 2007. Information Commons Discussion Group, Washington, D.C.

Kate Edger Information Commons Publications. http://www.information-commons.auckland.ac.nz/?page=publications.

University of Auckland Library, New Zealand.

McMullen, Susan. "The Learning Commons Model: Determining Best Practices for Design, Implementation, and Service." http://faculty.rwu.edu/smcmullen/site_visits.htm.

Information commons website created by librarian Susan McMullen during a sabbatical from Roger Williams University (Bristol, R.I.). Currently includes photos and information about Appalachian State University, Bridgewater State College, Brookdale Community College, Bucknell University, Connecticut College, Dickinson College, Duke University, Elon University, Hamilton College, Mount Holyoke College, Plymouth State University, Simmons College, SUNY Binghamton, SUNY Cortland, University of Massachusetts Amherst, University of North Carolina at Charlotte, University of Southern Maine, and Wesleyan University.

Murray, David. "Information Commons: A Directory of Innovative Services and Resources in Academic Libraries." http://ux.brookdalecc.edu/library/infocommons/ic_home.html.

Brookdale Community College, Lincroft, N.J. Updated through December 2004.

Slideshare. http://www.slideshare.net.

A place to share and discover PowerPoint presentations and slideshows on a wide range of library topics including information commons.

Books and Articles

Albanese, Andrew Richard. "Campus Library 2.0." *Library Journal* 129, no. 7 (2004): 30–33.

American Library Association, Library Administration and Management Association, Buildings and Equipment Sections, Functional Space Requirements Committee. *Building Blocks for Planning Functional Library Space*. Lanham, Md.: Scarecrow Press, 2001.

Bailey, Russell, and Barbara Tierney. "Information Commons Redux: Concept, Evolution, and Transcending the Tragedy of the Commons." *Journal of Academic Librarianship* 28, no. 5 (2002): 277–86.

Bazillion, Richard J., and Connie Braun. *Academic Libraries as High-Tech Gateways: A Guide to Design and Space Decisions.* Chicago: American Library Association, 1995.

———. "Academic Library Design: Building Teaching Instrument." *Computers in Libraries* 14, no. 2 (1994): 12–15.

Beagle, Donald. "Conceptualizing an Information Commons." *Journal of Academic Librarianship* 25, no. 2 (1999): 82–89.

———. "Extending the Information Commons: From Instructional Testbed to Internet2." *Journal of Academic Librarianship* 28, no. 5 (2002): 287–96.

Beagle, Donald (with contributions by Russ Bailey and Barbara Tierney). *The Information Commons Handbook.* New York: Neal-Schuman, 2006.

Bennett, Scott. *Libraries Designed for Learning.* Washington, D.C.: Council on Library and Information Resources, 2003. http://www.clir.org/pubs/abstract/pub122abst.html.

Bollier, David. "Why We Must Talk about the Information Commons." *Law Library Journal* 96, no. 2 (2004): 267–82.

Church, Jennifer. "The Evolving Information Commons." *Library Hi Tech* 23, no. 1 (2005): 75–81.

Church, Jennifer, Jason Vaughan, Wendy Starkweather, and Katherine Rankin. "The Information Commons at Lied Library (UNLV)." *Library Hi Tech* 20, no. 1 (2002): 58–70.

Cowgill, Allison, et al. "Implementing an Information Commons in a University Library." *Journal of Academic Librarianship* 27, no. 6 (2001): 432–39.

Crockett, Charlotte, et al. "Integrating Services in the Information Commons: Toward a Holistic Library and Computing Environment." *Library Administration and Management* 16, no. 4 (2002): 181–86.

Dallis, Diane. "Reference Services in the Commons Environment." *Reference Services Review* 34, no. 2 (2006): 248–60.

Demmers, Linda. "WebJunction's Focus on Space Planning for Libraries." Posted online on WebJunction, Jan. 31, 2006. http://webjunction.org/do/DisplayContent?id=12748.

Eckel, Peter, et al. *On Change III—Taking Charge of Change: A Primer for Colleges and Universities.* Washington, D.C.: American Council on Education, 2000. http://www.acenet.edu/bookstore/pdf/on-change/on-changeIII.pdf.

Ehrmann, Stephen C. "Beyond Computer Literacy: Implications of Technology for the Content of a College Education." *Liberal Education* 90, no. 4 (2004): 6–13.

"The Fate of the Undergraduate Library: Views of Six Librarians and One Faculty Member." *Library Journal* 125, no. 18 (2000): 38–41.

Gardner, Susan, and Susanna Eng. "What Students Want: Generation Y and the Changing Function of the Academic Library." *Libraries and the Academy* 5, no. 3 (2005): 405–29.

Green, Marybeth, and Daniel V. Eastmond. "The Information Commons: A Public Policy Report." *Quarterly Review of Distance Education* 6, no. 4 (2005): 409–13.

Haas, Leslie, et al. *The Information Commons.* SPEC Kit 281. Washington, D.C.: Association of Research Libraries, 2004.

Halbert, Martin. "Lessons from the Information Commons Frontier." *Journal of Academic Librarianship* 25, no. 2 (1999): 90–91.

Hardin, Garrett. "The Tragedy of the Commons." *Science* 161 (December 1968): 1243–48.

Holmes-Wong, Deborah, et al. "If You Build It, They Will Come: Spaces, Values, and Services in the Digital Era." *Library Administration and Management* 11, no. 2 (1997): 74–85.

Huber, Mary Taylor, and Pat Hutchings. "Building the Teaching Commons." *Change* 38, no. 3 (2006): 24–31.

Hughes, Carol Ann. "Facework: A New Role for the Next Generation of Library-Based Information Technology Centers." *Library Hi Tech* 16, nos. 3–4 (1998): 27–35.

———. "Information Services for Higher Education: A New Competitive Space." *D-Lib Magazine*

6, no. 12 (2000). Text version available at http://www.dlib.org/dlib/december00/hughes/12hughes.html#ref29.

Kratz, Charles. "Transforming the Delivery of Service: The Joint-Use Library and Information Commons." *College and Research Libraries News* 64, no. 2 (2003): 100–101. http://www.ala.org/ala/acrl/acrlpubs/crlnews/backissues2003/february1/transforming.cfm.

Lee, D. R. "Constructing the Commons: Practical Projects to Build the Information Commons." *Knowledge Quest* 31, no. 4 (2003): 13–15.

"Libraries Replacing Books with Bytes." *Information Management Journal* 39, no. 4 (2005): 13.

Lippincott, Joan K. "New Library Facilities: Opportunities for Collaboration." *Resource Sharing and Information Networks* 17, nos. 1–2 (2004): 147–57.

Lowry, Anita. "The Information Arcade at the University of Iowa." *Cause/Effect* 17, no. 3 (1994): 38–44.

MacWhinnie, L. A. "The Information Commons: the Academic Library of the Future." *Portal: Libraries and the Academy* 3, no. 2 (2003): 241–57.

Malenfant, Chuck. "The Information Commons as a Collaborative Workspace." *Reference Services Review* 34, no. 2 (2006): 279–86.

Mangan, Katherine S. "Packing Up the Books." *Chronicle of Higher Education* 51, no. 43 (2005): A27–A28.

Miller, Michael. "Anticipating the Future: The University of Michigan's Media Union." *Library Hi Tech* 16, no. 1 (1998): 71–83.

Oblinger, Diana. "Leading the Transition from Classrooms to Learning Spaces." *EDUCAUSE Quarterly* 28, no. 1 (2005): 14–18.

———, ed. *Learning Spaces*. Boulder, Colo.: EDUCAUSE, 2006. http://www.educause.edu/learningspaces/.

Oblinger, Diane, and James L. Oblinger, eds. *Educating the Net Generation*. Boulder, Colo.: EDUCAUSE, 2005. http://www.educause.edu/educatingthenetgen/.

Orgeron, Elizabeth. "Integrated Academic Student Support Services at Loyola University: The Library as a Resource Clearinghouse." *Journal of Southern Academic and Special Librarianship* 2, no.

3 (2001). http://southernlibrarianship.icaap.org/content/v02n03/orgeron_e01.htm.

Pierce, Jennifer Burek. "Next Stop, Information Commons." *American Libraries* 35, no. 4 (2004): 87.

Rao, Robert, et al. "Public Access to Information and the Creation of an 'Information Commons.'" *Proceedings of the 76th ASIS&T Annual Meeting,* vol. 41 (2004): 198ff.

Schader, Barbara. *Learning Commons: Evolution and Collaborative Essentials*. Oxford: Chandos, 2007.

Spencer, Mary Ellen. "Evolving a New Model: The Information Commons." *Reference Services Review* 34, no. 2 (2006): 242–47.

Tompkins, Philip. "New Structures for Teaching Libraries." *Library Administration and Management* 4 (Spring 1990): 71–81.

Wamken, Paula. "New Technologies and Constant Change: Managing the Process." *Journal of Academic Librarianship* 30, no. 4 (2004): 322–27.

Whitchurch, Michael. "Information Commons at Brigham Young University: Past, Present, and Future." *Reference Services Review* 34, no. 2 (2006): 261–78.

White, Peggy, Susan Beatty, and Darlene Warren. "Information Commons," in *Encyclopedia of Library and Information Science*. New York: Marcel Dekker, 2004. http://www.dekker.com/servlet/product/DOI/101081EELIS120020359.

Wilson, Lizabeth A. "Collaborate or Die: Designing Library Space." *ARL Bimonthly Report* 222 (2002). http://www.arl.org/newsltr/222/collabwash.html.

Presentations

Acker, Stephen R., and Michael D. Miller. "Stewardship of the Information Commons: Cultural, Service, and Operational Issues." Presented at EDUCAUSE Annual Conference, 2004. (ID: EDU0479).

Bailey, Russell. "Information Commons Services for Learners and Researchers: Evolution in Patron Needs, Digital Resources and Scholarly Publishing." Presented at INFORUM 2005, Prague, Czech Republic. http://www.inforum

.cz/inforum2005/english/prispevek.phppri-spevek=32.htm.

Beagle, Donald. "From Information Commons to Learning Commons." Presented at Leavey Library, University of Southern California, Sept. 16–17, 2004 Conference. "Information Commons: Learning Space beyond the Classroom." http://www.usc.edu/isd/libraries/locations/leavey/news/conference/presentations/presentations_9-16/Beagle_Information_Commons_to_Learning.pdf.

Beatty, Susan. "The Information Commons at the University of Calgary: Strategies for Integration." PowerPoint slides from a presentation at the first International Conference on IT and Information Literacy in Glasgow, March, 2002. http://www.iteu.gla.ac.uk/elit/itilit2002/papers/ppt/06.ppt.

Cowgill, Allison. "The Information Commons Challenge." PowerPoint slides from a presentation at the American Library Association's MARS Chair's Program in Toronto, June 22, 2003. http://www.iub.edu/~librcsd/mars/2003annual/MARS2003Cowgill.ppt.

"Elements of an Information Commons. . . ." EDUCAUSE 2005 Workshop Presented at EDUCAUSE in Australasia 2005 Conference, Auckland, Australia. http://www.educause2005.auckland.ac.nz/interactive/presentations/3%20Elements%20and%20collaboration.pdf.

Gjelten, Daniel R., et al. "The Architecture of an Idea: The Information Commons and the Future of the Academic Library." Presented at EDUCAUSE Annual Conferences, 2004. (ID: EDU4107)

Mountifield, Hester M. "Learning . . . with a Latte. The Kate Edger Information Commons—providing student-centred learning support." Presented at EDUCAUSE in Australasia 2003 Conference, Adelaide, Australia. http://www.information-commons.auckland.ac.nz/content_files/publications/educause_article.pdf.

Stoan, Steve. "The Library as an Instrument for Teaching and Learning." Presented at the 2002 Workshop on the Transformation of the College Library, Council of Independent Colleges Conference (Sept. 19–21, 2002), Columbia, Maryland. http://www.cic.edu/conferences_events/workshop/library/2002/steve_stoan.asp.

Other Publications, Reports, Papers

ACRL. 2003 ACRL Environmental Scan. (members only) http://www.ala.org/ala/acrl/acrlpubs/whitepapers/whitepapersreports.htm.

ACRL conducts an ongoing environmental scan to identify trends and emerging issues that may affect the future of higher education, academic libraries, and the association. This the most recent version of the scan. This information is password protected for ACRL members only.

————. Guidelines for Media Resources in Academic Libraries. 2006. Available at http://www.ala.org/ala/acrl/acrlstandards/mediaresources.htm.

Cain, David, and Gary L. Reynolds. "The Impact of Facilities on Recruitment and Retention of Students." 2007.

Executive summary of the authors' research project sponsored by APPA's Center for Facilities Research. Part I: http://www.appa.org/FacilitiesManager/article.cfm?ItemNumber=2567&parentid=254. Part II: http://www.appa.org/FacilitiesManager/article.cfm?ItemNumber=2587&parentid=2544.

Freeman, Geoffrey E., et al. "Library as Place: Rethinking Roles, Rethinking Space." Council on Library and Information Resources, publication 129 (Feb. 2005). http://www.clir.org/pubs/abstract/pub129abst.html.

Horizon Report, a collaboration between the New Media Consortium and the EDUCAUSE Learning Initiative. NMC, 2006. http://www.nmc.org/horizon/.

King, Helen. "The Academic Library in the 21st Century: What Need for a Physical Place?" IATUL (International Assoc. of Technological University Libraries) Proceedings, ns 10 (2000). http://iatul.org/doclibrary/public/Conf_Proceedings/2000/King.rtf.

Malone, Debbie, Bethany Levrault, and Michael J. Miller. "Factors Influencing the Number of Computers in Libraries: An Exploratory White Paper." ACRL, 2006. http://www.ala.org/ala/acrl/aboutacrl/acrlsections/collegelibraries/collpubs/white_paper_computers_in_libraries_april2006.pdf.

Index

Note: Page numbers in bold indicate case studies. Page numbers in italics indicate photographs.

Donald Russell Bailey, Providence College, and **Barbara Gunter Tierney**, UNC Charlotte, are nationally recognized authorities on information commons. From 2001 to 2005, Bailey served as the associate university librarian of the Information Commons at the University of North Carolina at Charlotte. Currently, he is the library director at Providence College in Rhode Island. This author team has given programs on information commons ranging from its planning, implementing, and assessing to the practical nuts and bolts. They have also written books together concerning information commons.

Printed in the United States
221465BV00001B/2/P